Terry Gould, Judith Brierley
& Kathy Coates-Mohammed

LEARNING AND PLAYING
INDOORS

How to create an inspiring indoor environment

Published 2012 by Featherstone Education
Bloomsbury Publishing plc
50 Bedford Square, London,
www.acblack.com

ISBN 978-1-4081-5549-3

Text © Terry Gould, Judith Brierley & Kathy Coates-Mohammed 2012
Design © Lynda Murray
Photographs © Shutterstock

Printed in Great Britain by Latimer Trend & Company Ltd

This book is produced using paper that is made from wood grown in
managed, sustainable forests. It is natural, renewable and recyclable.
The logging and manufacturing processes conform to the environmental
regulations of the country of origin.

To see our full range of titles visit www.acblack.com

Acknowledgements
Many thanks to the children, practitioners and parents from St Patrick's RC Primary
School, Manchester; Medlock Primary School, Manchester; Kids Unlimited, Timperley;
Kids Unlimited, Warrington; Little Hulton Sure Start Children's Centre, Salford; Old Hall
Drive Primary School, Manchester; Acorn Childcare Ltd, Milton Keynes, and Peter Ellse
and the staff at Cosy Ltd of Derby whose photographic images are used throughout this
book.

Contents

Preface

Over many years Kathy, Judith and I have, through our roles as consultants/advisory teachers, provided advice to a great number of early years and Year 1 practitioners on how to develop, resource and maintain their early years indoor learning environments. The advice we have provided has been practical, useful and proven to be highly effective. In the book The Fabulous Early Years Foundation Stage (Featherstone Education) I allude to my identified 'five pillars' which I feel underpin all early years provision:

- **A quality, positive, learning environment – indoors and outdoors**

- **Observation, recording and assessment**

- **Planning**

- **Learning and teaching**

- **Partnership with parents**

Following the review of the EYFS, and the resultant changes to it which reinforce the effect of the learning environment on young children's progress and development, it makes sense that we should put this advice into a printed format that is accessible to practitioners, not only from across the United Kingdom but from around the world . This book is intended to support guidance provided by local authority advisers and consultants; particularly at a time where the local authority role is changing radically due to the current economic climate and new ways of working. In some cases where local authority support is limited or not available, this book may well provide a critical level of guidance to enable settings to develop and improve their provision.

We believe that this book will also be useful to those seeking to bring their practice and provision in line with the new Early Years framework requirements (DfE 2012). We hope it will be helpful not only to early year's practitioners but to leaders, managers, advisory teachers, consultants, head teachers and students alike. We would like to express our thanks to the children, practitioners and parents from St Patrick's RC Primary School, Manchester; Medlock Primary School, Manchester; Kids Unlimited, Timperley; Kids Unlimited, Warrington; Little Hulton Sure Start Children's Centre, Salford; Old Hall Drive Primary School, Manchester; Acorn Childcare Ltd, Milton Keynes, and Peter Ellse and the staff at Cosy Ltd of Derby whose photographic images are used throughout this book. We hope they will all enjoy reading this book and seeing themselves featured in it.

Terry Gould , Judith Brierley and Kathy Coates-Mohammed
April 2012

The importance of the learning environment

"Though they do not know as much about the world as most adults, children know how they feel and what is important to them."

Judy Miller (Never too Young: Save the Children 2003)

The importance of early education has been recognised for many years. However, it is only in relatively recent years that attention in this country has become particularly and significantly focused on the importance of the learning environment. Little formal guidance has been provided through statutory frameworks and it has been mainly left to local authorities and other training providers to support settings so as to ensure that what is offered to children is stimulating, motivating and meaningful. The period from birth to 5 years is an optimum time of rapid growth, both physically and intellectually, and the right kind of provision through a high quality learning environment can help to bring about highly beneficial outcomes for all children. Given that the young child at this age is…

* **a naturally active learner operating most effectively through first-hand experience**

* **naturally curious to investigate but also at times needing this to be encouraged, stimulated and nurtured**

* **likely to gain great benefit from interaction with others**

…then the importance of providing the best quality provision cannot be underestimated.

A non-negotiable must!

Practitioners may at times question why they have to make such an effort to develop and deliver quality provision and when at their lowest, sometimes their inner voice kicks in with 'why bother?' When this happens, it's time to really worry because it signals a lack of understanding, a lack of commitment and a lack of vision. It may signal other things as well, such as the setting not effectively self-evaluating or working as a team. Hopefully, this book will enable many obstacles, myths and concerns to be overcome so that an indoor environment can be created which is exciting and challenging and which supports and extends each child's learning and development. It is a 'non-negotiable must' that children are provided with a carefully considered, skilfully presented, stimulating and positive environment that is inclusive and encourages a range of play, exploration, problem solving and talk activities. Children need to be able to independently choose, create, investigate, explore, initiate and persevere with activities.

Substantial benefits will only be accrued if the learning environment is of the highest quality and supports good learning, both independently and with/alongside others. There is therefore a heavy responsibility for leaders and managers of early years settings to ensure that this is made into a reality through leading the staff team forward towards excellence in every aspect of their provision including the indoor environment. The newly identified prime areas of learning and development: Personal, social and emotional development, Physical development and Communication and language will each be greatly supported by an inclusive, positive, indoor environment which provides a 'wow factor' for children, along with being accessible and stage appropriate. A similar scenario is equally applicable to activities within the specific areas: Literacy, Mathematics, Understanding of the world and Expressive arts and design.

It is every practitioner's responsibility, led by the setting's manager, to provide an environment which supports, stimulates and structures both child-initiated and adult-led learning. Indeed, it is the right of every child to be cared for and educated by suitably qualified and experienced adults who have a clear understanding of how children learn, and importantly an adult who understands the key role the learning environment plays in this. For example if quality books are presented in an attractive book area for children, one which attracts their interest and where they can comfortably 'snuggle up' with a book, then they will want to engage with books, become interested in the words and pictures and become motivated to learn to read for themselves.

What is going to be required under the revised framework (DfE 2012) is that early years settings **must** ensure that all children's learning and development is maximised, and they are provided with the best possible start; particularly where they come from a disadvantaged background. To meet the new requirements, practitioners need to ensure that the indoor environment is positive and inclusive and is underpinned by guiding principles including:

- **It enables all identified/required areas of learning and development to be supported and accessed, both prime and specific**

- **It is meaningful, motivating and interesting to children**

- **It is adapted and enhanced in line with children's identified developing interests and needs on an ongoing basis**

- **It is offered alongside a high quality, positive, easily accessible outdoor learning environment**

- **It is structured and maintained so that all learning spaces and resources are easily accessible and appropriately used by the children**

- **It offers cosy, defined and attractively developed spaces where children are inspired to actively play and learn independently and with an appropriate level of adult guidance and support**

Although the revised EYFS does not focus on the four themes in exactly the same way as the previous framework (DfE 2007), it does identify **Four Overarching Principles** (Dfe 2012):

- **Every child is a unique child, who is constantly learning and can be resilient, capable, confident and self-assured;**

- **Children learn to be strong and independent through positive relationships**

- **Children learn and develop well in enabling environments, in which their experiences respond to their individual needs and there is a strong partnership between practitioners and parents and/or carers; and**

- **Children develop and learn in different ways and at different rates. The framework covers the education and care of all children in early years provision, including children with special educational needs and disabilities.**

The rate of progress in learning and development made by all children is one quantitative way of measuring the quality of what is provided and this, significantly, includes the learning environment.

There are two main strands of evidence type to consider around early years provision:

1 **Qualitative** - relating to, measuring, or measured by the quality (size, appearance, value etc.) of something rather than its quantity.

2 **Quantitative** - relating to, measuring, or measured by the quantity of something and evidenced by data.

The strength and quality of the learning environment indoors comes under the qualitative strand. The indoor environment is key to ensuring that opportunities within all areas of learning and development are provided at an adequate and appropriate level and should reflect the fact that all these areas are equally important and are inter-connected.

From the five pillars mentioned in the preface, I have developed a further set of ten comprehensive key principles that between them qualitatively and quantitatively underpin, not just the environment-based aspect of provision dealt with in this book, but all aspects of the new early years provision and practice requirements (DfE 2012). You will see that in many ways each overlaps with the other and each is in some way inter-dependent on the others. When focused on for self-evaluation purposes, these ten principles can help a setting to become outstanding or to maintain that status.

This book will particularly focus on the requirements of the revised EYFS framework and my identified principle number one relating to '**A quality, positive learning environment**' and my principles, numbers four and five, relating to '**Welfare**' and '**Effective learning and teaching**' but will naturally, in some ways, have links to each of the other seven identified principles.

My ten identified key underpinning principles are:

1

A QUALITY, POSITIVE LEARNING ENVIRONMENT
(Indoors and outdoors)
Space, time, materials and emotional well-being are planned and organised to give children the best opportunity to learn and develop, through among other things, exploring, experimenting and making appropriate decisions for themselves, enabling them to learn at their own developmental level and pace whilst ensuring they are kept safe and healthy.

2

PARENT CARER PARTNERSHIP
All practitioners develop strong and supportive parent/carer partnerships, ensuring an atmosphere within which children have security and confidence and where parental understanding and support is developed and fostered right from the start.

3

TEAMWORK
The staff operate as a whole team, developing collaborative ways of working with motivational levels heightened, and support provided for professional development by learning from each other: thus strengthening the ethos and pedagogical approach in the setting, including effective transitions into, across, and beyond the setting.

4

WELFARE
Children are kept safe and healthy through a range of good practice experiences identified through policies, including appropriate on-going risk assessments, healthy food and drinks, opportunities for appropriate physical exercise, safe guarding practices, the employment of suitable people etc.

5

EFFECTIVE LEARNING AND TEACHING
The provision will have created broad opportunities across all seven areas of learning in the new EYFS Framework. There will be appropriate opportunities for differentiation to meet children's individual learning needs, their emotional well being and their uniqueness, which ensure continuity and progression of learning through building on what children already know and can do. The role of the adult, including the key person, is strong and well developed so as to support high quality interactions with children, developing children's language and communication skills, and enabling them to make a positive contribution.

6

STRONG SCHOOL/SETTING LINKS

The school/setting will have strong links with future feeder schools/settings which effectively support a successful transition process for the benefit of the children involved, and which is based on all staff having a clear understanding of its purpose and value.

7

OBSERVATION, RECORDING AND PLANNING

A continuous process of observation is in place informing planning. This is led by the knowledge of all members of the team as to how children most effectively learn and develop and is supported by high quality records of children's learning and development.

8

ASSESSMENT

Detailed formal and informal/incidental observations are used to make formative and summative assessments including identifying the next steps for individual children to ensure continuity and maximisation of their learning and development. These are updated regularly and shared with children parents/carers.

9

TRAINING AND STAFF DEVELOPMENT

All staff are supported at a level that takes them forward individually and as a team. Effective performance management systems support improved practice and outcomes for all children. Training and development provided has clear and strong links to the setting's development plans.

10

MANAGEMENT

Leadership and management is strong and focused ensuring that they are able to effectively lead the setting forward towards continuous improvement leading to outstanding outcomes for all. Managers/leaders receive appropriate training and external support and keep abreast of current research, legislation and developments in the early years.

Education and care are inseparable

My identified principle number four is about 'welfare', a key aspect identified by the new early years requirement (DfE 2012), and it is essential that all the staff team truly appreciate that education and care are inseparable. You cannot have good quality education without good quality care and vice versa. Hence the physical environment should be seen as supporting care through emotional well being. Every aspect of the environment can make a significant contribution to both the cognitive development and the emotional well-being of the child. There can be no justification for creating artificial barriers between education and care. This was recognised by the original EYFS guidance framework (DfE 2007) and is again recognised by the revised EYFS framework (DfE 2012). Good quality care is vitally important whatever the age of the young child but the younger the child the even more important it is.

Quality observations

Whatever is provided by the setting must be sensitive and responsive and as such informed by imaginative and empathetic understanding of the feelings and experiences of the child. Practitioners working with all ages/stages of children must closely and systematically observe children at play and engaged in active learning and then use this to inform their future practice. Information so gathered should be shared and discussed, as appropriate, with colleagues and parents/carers and where of significance, recorded through children's learning journeys and written development records. The key person system, heuristic/sensory play and outdoor experiences are particularly relevant to this for babies, toddlers and rising three year olds.

Editor's notes

In Chapter 2, readers will embark on a journey towards creating a learning environment but the messages from Chapter 1 need to be held onto within that journey, as well as the important new messages that are brought forward. As the book unravels the reader will find even more answers to the question 'why bother?'. The role of the adult is crucial to the success of the provision and for this reason this is dealt with in more detail in Chapter 5 and will be supported through the use of the audits in Chapter 8.

Chapter 2

Towards a quality learning environment -

Creating a place to learn with the "wow factor"

> "Places Speak! Places do not leave us indifferent. They reflect what we think about children, parents/carers and educators."
>
> (Carla Rinaldi - Reggio Emilia)

This powerful and inspirational quote is fundamentally useful in guiding the creation of any vision for an effective and stimulating early years environment. This is because the moment anyone, child or adult, enters the learning environment they are receiving messages – messages from the things they see, the way the space is organised, the resources they are presented with and how these are presented as well as the way the session/day is organised. But these messages don't stop there because they are part of a two way communication process. Places 'speak' to us and the children and practitioners get messages back from the children, including the things we hear them say and see them doing. These are the ways the children communicate with each other and with practitioners. Messages also come to us from self reflecting on the way we feel about the quality/wow factor of what we provide; the values and the inseparable education and care permeating throughout our environment.

> "The premises and equipment must be organised in a way that meets the needs of children."
>
> (DfE 2012)

The learning environment is at the very heart of the early years educator's practice, so much so that it feels almost fundamentally a reflection of the whole reason for ourselves and the children being there. Yes, places really do 'speak' to children and adults and this poses several reflective questions for all early years educators.

When and how do you find/make the time to stand back and observe your environment, to look, listen and feel your environment, to think about your ethos? You need to do this on an ongoing basis and at these times you can ask yourself questions such as:

- **What messages does my environment give to the children and parents?**

- **Have we appropriately engaged in professional dialogue as a team to create an ethos that underpins and permeates the environment on offer?**

- **Do we all as a team have a shared knowledge and understanding about what we provide and why, and are we all in agreement?**

- **Do children and parents/carers feel the same way about our environment as we do?**

- **Do we reflect on and evaluate our environment regularly enough and in enough detail?**

We know from experience that each setting/school community is different. Alongside this, we should also recognise that the environment we create should reflect the uniqueness of community we serve. As such, it then makes sense that the environment will be different in each setting. We must get away from the myth that each environment will be the same, as if there is a blueprint to be accessed and used. There isn't one! Each environment has its own physical space and through this its own strengths and its own challenges. Focusing on the positive aspects of each challenging space will make the creative process an enjoyable and celebratory one. The ultimate goal is to create an enabling environment, which will continue to evolve in an embryonic way with no final perfect ending! As an effective, positive, enabling environment it should be continually changing in line with the children's needs and interests. In this way, every environment in every setting is unique and ever changing.

Creating a whole team shared vision

> "Practitioners must consider the individual needs, interests, and stage of development of each child in their care, and must use this information to plan a challenging and enjoyable experience for each child in all of the areas of learning and development."
>
> (DfE 2012)

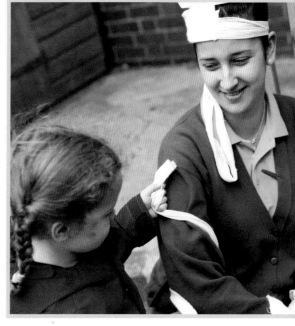

It is critically important that a shared vision is developed amongst the whole team, ensuring that each practitioner has a clear knowledge and understanding of the vision for the environment and each feels their ideas and opinions are valued.

It's a good idea to visit other settings, together as a team if possible, where there already exists a quality learning environment so as to gain ideas and see first-hand what works for different physical spaces. Ask if you can take photographs to share back at your setting later to inform your team discussions, remembering that every environment is unique and what works for one physical space does not necessarily work for every environment. You cannot transpose one environment directly onto another.

Where possible, try to involve children and parents in your discussions about what things they would like to see in their environment. Children often have very clear ideas and opinions about which resources they like to access on a permanent basis and which learning spaces/workshops they want only sometimes (flexible spaces). Read up on indoor environments by sourcing relevant articles and books, and plan time for whole team discussions around some of these.

Getting there

How then are we going to achieve, what we might term, this 'Quality, enabling learning environment' for our young children? What key elements do we need to consider?

Perhaps the first thing to consider is that we need to view the environment as if through the eyes of a child. This can best be experienced by getting down to a child's level and asking yourself if what you see is appropriate for each and every one of your children's learning needs? Most often, this is effectively done as a whole team through a 'learning walk' of the environment, with discussions taking place during and afterwards which lead to points of action agreed and to be addressed. It's about creating a team vision and a team understanding of the issues involved.

Using your observations to see and feel the environment you want for your children is a powerful tool towards creating the environment required; one that 'speaks' the messages of caring, being safe, being inviting, and a stimulating, exciting place to play and learn indoors!

The entrance area to the setting

Remember you only get one chance to create a good first impression so spend some time reflecting on the entrance area to your building. This area is of key importance as it is the first space children, parents/carers and visitors will see on arrival and the last thing as they leave. Your entrance area needs to make the best use of whatever space you have available and should:

- **be well lit including as much natural light much as possible**

- **have comfortable chairs and tables for waiting parents**

- **have suitable, attractive floor covering**

- **have one or more large plants**

- **have suitable soothing background music playing**

- **have a small amount of interesting play resources accessible, to be engaged with by young children who might be waiting with parents/carers**

- **have on display information for parents/carers such as session times and menus, for instance, on a wall display which includes a welcome sign**

- **have on display A4 or A3 sized laminated photos of children playing to learn with informative descriptors/comments. These images could also alternatively or additionally be displayed on a wall mounted TV screen or a digital photo frame**

- **have a visitors' book**

- **have an easily accessible visitor's toilet close by**

Overall, whatever you create must be a genuinely welcoming space which is pleasant to pass through or to wait in. Remember, it is after all a public statement about your provision and as such needs to 'speak' to your clients in positive ways. Don't forget too that it will be the first indoor space that any Ofsted inspector will see on the day of your inspection.

Things to bear in mind:

- **too many notices and loose papers pinned on boards can give it an institutional or uncared for look**

- **grubby or tatty, uncared for, flooring will hardly impress**

- **the staff who meet and greet visitors are also part of the entrance area environment**

- **how it smells is important too**

- **keep it a calm space as any excessive noise in the entrance area is not a helpful ingredient to feeling comfortable and relaxed**

Chapter 3

A focus on the environment – babies, toddlers and pre-school children

"There is a clear need to provide all our children with high quality care encompassed within high quality educational content"

(Osborne & Melbank 1987)

The context of any daycare provision for babies and toddlers and pre-school children is set in the fullness and richness of the environment provided, the structure and organisation through which it is accessed and the underpinning ethos. Adults are a key part of that environment and hence staffing really matters, both numbers and quality wise.

Staffing matters

Both adult/child ratios and the quality of staff themselves are a key part of the provision and effectiveness the environment can have on outcomes for the child. *'The higher the staff ration the better the care'* is a recognised saying which often has much truth within it. This is the reason why the revised EYFS is setting new standards in terms of qualifications and experience for staff working with young children. But merely being present is never going to be enough and it is what the practitioners actually do, and the quality of the attention they give to individual babies, toddlers and pre-schoolers that matters. Two major reasons for this being the case are, firstly, the children's recurring need for love, care, attention and stimulation and secondly, their developing capacity for communication. Overall, research tells us that the more responsive the adults then the better cognitive and language outcomes for children; as well as the higher the levels of emotional well-being that are achieved. To make all of the above into a reality, settings need to ensure that among other things:

- furniture is of the right size and shape

- soft furnishings such as cushions, curtains, rugs and blinds are well maintained and are of a colour harmonious to the eye

- floor coverings are of an appropriate style which can be easily kept clean and are well maintained

- there is a feeling of space but also cosiness

- resources are carefully selected to support recognised learning and development outcomes and are age/stage appropriate

The way allocated funding for resources, and time away from the children, is spent is most important and we must not allow any under-funding (of time or money) to lead to our very youngest children spending their formative years surrounded by what in some instances can only described as 'ugliness, tat and clutter'. As visiting consultants, all too often we see poor quality or torn books badly stored, tatty and/or grubby soft toys piled high in the corner or elsewhere and other resources poorly displayed and stored. As well as this we see walls of settings 'decorated' with giant cartoon characters and pictures painted on the windows of teddy bears and Disney characters. These do nothing or very little for the appearance of the room/building and contribute nothing to the children's learning and development outcomes. They represent what might be termed 'the tacky element' of former times, and more often than not reduce the light coming into the room and being reflected throughout the space. Much better, subject to wall space, to have:

- a few good paintings reflecting the culture of the area on some of the walls

- a range of A4 or A3 size laminated photos or canvas prints of children, with suitable explanations/comments where possible sited at child height

- an attractive noticeboard for parents and visitors

- displays which help to define the learning spaces

Whatever you do, you must remember that you will need to give attention to the visual aspects of the environment on an ongoing basis.

The decor

Whether it's a new or existing environment it's always best to stick to plain/neutral wall and ceiling paint colours that are not too bright, so that wall displays, hangings, mobiles, pictures, drapes and soft furnishings can then be used creatively to bring in the colour to the space. Floor coverings need to be cosy, comfortable to sit on and noise absorbent and may be a mixture between fitted carpets or rugs and wipe clean surfaces such as cushion flooring. Whilst fully carpeted has been the traditional choice in the past, an increasing number of settings are now moving away from this to a wipe clean surface overall with rugs strategically placed in appropriate places. Rugs can be very easily machine washed or dry cleaned and wipe clean surfaces steam mopped. By opting for wipe clean surfaces and rugs the space remains more flexible and the room can more easily be rearranged/adjusted, as well as the messes that little children make being that much easier to clean up quickly and without fuss. Having said that, you do have to be careful that the rugs or mats provided offer a degree of quality, and a level of co-ordination of colour. So it is better to use just one or two colours of rug rather than an over bright mish-mash of many colours.

Organising and maintaining

The way in which rooms/areas are organised can make a real difference to independent access to resources and for child-initiated activity to take place. NB: it must not be seen as a one off that once done is forgotten! All practitioners working with babies and toddlers and pre-schoolers have to cope with the dilemma of keeping the space tidy. Here the challenge is not to be almost obsessively tidying up all the time or every time something gets moved out of place, it is about getting the balance right and keeping the room/space in reasonable order.

We would all recognise that the lack of floor and storage space, along with the constant moving of resources, and sometimes furniture, by children can feel very trying at times. As long as it remains stimulating, attractive to the children and safe are the main things to remember and focus on. How you store resources and what you have accessible at any one time will dictate how much of a mess they get into. The old adage 'less is more' applies here. For example in the baby room it is better to have three or four sensory objects with silhouette place holders on top of a very low level storage unit, than half a dozen small tubs with a number of things in that will simply be tipped up by more mobile babies as they access them. To enable practitioners to be facilitators of learning and development, storage should be in appropriate, low level, open shelving so enabling children to access things easily and safely and able to see what is available and if necessary communicate their desire for it.

It is best to be selective about the number of mobiles, decorations and pictures/paintings on the walls. Here again, less is more. Someone in the room needs to take on the responsibility for co-ordinating any wall displays otherwise these can quickly become uncared for and of a mixed quality – a kind of confusing conglomeration!

One good idea when planning the space is to observe children's overall movement and attention during different times of the day/session. This will often identify 'dead' areas, which are hardly ever used for free access, causing more crowding in other areas. Issues identified as a result of your observations can then be addressed.

Getting the feel right

Close your eyes and imagine that you are the parent of a young child. You are about to entrust the most precious thing in your life to the care of others. It is a mighty decision to take – choosing the people and an environment that you can trust.

Now in your mind, walk into your ideal nursery room. Summon up in your imagination, using all your senses, just what makes it special. Why are you choosing this place, rather than any other, for your child? Write down just four key words on a piece of paper that you feel capture the nature, look, and feel of the environment that will help to nurture your child. I can guess that for some they might include words such as 'warmth' or 'stimulating'. But you should select the words that are most suitable for you! Then using these share them with each other and come up with four words you can all agree on as a team. These words should now form the bedrock of your team journey to designing and creating the rooms for the babies and toddlers in your care. Whilst you read this part of the book, take some time to reflect and work on your room. Stand back at various points of the day and reflect. Ensure that what you are shaping and providing is putting into practice the vision that you have just created.

Young children learn about the world around them by using all their senses. The environment we create should capitalise on this by giving them the opportunity to engage with objects and materials in a highly tactile and multi-sensory manner. By giving them the freedom to explore using not only their sight, but with touch, smell, hearing and taste as well, we are creating links and patterns of understanding in their brains. When designing workshop areas for babies, toddlers and pre-schoolers, think loosely and in more open ended ways, in different ways than you have done previously. Try to think how you can use baskets and chests, where possible, to contain and display resources. But we also need to think how we can make these as accessible as we can. For example, one idea for the babies (perhaps those just able to sit unaided), is to fill a play ring or ball pool with resources and encourage them to sit within it and explore. Objects can be hung from a baby gym type frame for the youngest to engage with. Don't expect the resources you provide to stay in one place though because they won't! Children will travel and along with them the resources. This is a sign of them transferring their learning and making further links between experiences.

The building

The physical environment can exert a major influence on how practitioners working with babies, toddlers and pre-schoolers feel about their work as well as the quality of experiences with which the children are able to engage.

The building itself needs to be suitable for purpose, warm and inviting to children and parents/carers. Even new builds as well as older buildings can be cold, sterile and institutional in their outward impression. Whatever we start with we must ensure that we make this into an environment which is comfortable and attractive to both children and adults. It has to combine comfort and homeliness with practicability.

In the baby room

Babies need an indoor environment rich with opportunities to explore. 'Home from home' spaces all set up and resourced with a clear understanding that a good deal of the touching, mouthing, banging, patting and throwing of toys is done to test the nature and properties of objects. For very young children the emotional environment is of paramount importance. They need to feel safe, loved and secure so practitioners need to create cosy spaces where the key person can feed a baby, cuddle up or spend special time interacting and playing. The furniture should be chosen to support the physical development of the children; to encourage crawling and early supported walking skills – and to divide the room into smaller exciting areas.

A good quality baby room environment will have many characteristics such as:

- **spaces which are clean but have the capacity to become messy**

- **resources which may imitate home. e.g comfy chairs to sit on with their key person**

- **a safe and secure environment which includes ensuring appropriate room temperatures, ventilation, boundaries, natural light and displaying photos of families**

- **spaces for routine activities such as snack time and exploratory play**

- **stimulating resources that cater for all of the senses**

- **a quiet, comfortable and safe environment to sleep and rest**

- **space available for parents and carers to access and to talk with staff**

- **appropriately sized furniture which is safe for babies to navigate**

- **a variety of textures, levels and surfaces**

- **regular, and where possible direct, access to the outdoor learning environment**

- **provision enhanced on an ongoing basis according to children's developmental needs, interests and on-going observations made by staff**

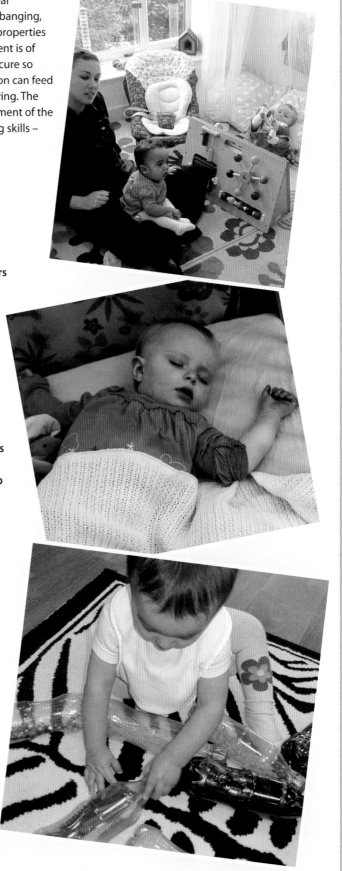

Reflecting on practice is a crucial element of effective provision and is much encouraged by the renewed EYFS framework. It will help to further develop the quality of the provision and the experiences that are offered to the children. The following are examples of the type of questions you may like to consider to support your self-reflection:

- Is the room warm and welcoming for the babies?

- What do the parents think of it on behalf of their baby?

- What can a baby see when lying on his/her stomach or back?

- What does the surface the babies are lying/crawling on feel like?

- Are there mirrors for the babies to see themselves in and so develop a sense of self esteem?

- How effectively and purposefully do staff interact with all the babies?

- How do staff communicate and share ideas with parents/carers?

- How do staff observe babies and then use the information to further enhance the environment and learning and development opportunities?

Learning spaces

The following learning spaces are those which baby room staff should develop, resource and maintain to create an environment which is cosy and welcoming:

The sleeping/rest space

This space is best developed using neutral, warm colours to provide a calm, relaxing environment. The nappy changing area should include washable toys and mobiles to engage and comfort the children. It is most important that any sleeping and changing routines reflect those in the home. To best cater for the children's emotional and learning needs, whenever possible, it should be the key person who manages these care routines for the child. If you do not have the luxury of a separate area for sleep then you'll need to look carefully at the space on offer and think creatively about 'zoning off' an area of the room to provide a soft, inviting and cosy area for rest. Adequate sleep and rest are critical for a child's development and well-being; this area is therefore just as important to plan as the more stimulating, active ones.

Some ideas to consider

◆ **Sound travels:** How can you prevent children being disturbed whilst others play? Could you use… space dividers? Curtains? Soft surfaces (e.g. carpets, cushion floor and cushions all help to muffle noise)? Music softly playing that can engage the senses and distort other noise?

◆ **Lighting:** Will there be a glare from windows or lighting fixtures? Ideally the area needs subdued and soft lighting. Could you have… lamps on the wall? Coloured filters/bulbs? Curtains or blinds or dark cellophane panels at the windows? Glow in the dark plug sockets and projectors?

◆ **Use the ceiling:** Nothing too stimulating, but enough to provide a cosy and soft environment. Could you hang… mobiles, drapes or streamers?

◆ **Comforters:** How do you reflect home? Could you… have children's blankets and toys from home sitting on their beds/cots? Make it home-like by including rocking chairs, settees and cushions in the area?

◆ **Above all carefully consider the space where the children sleep.** It is absolutely essential that careful thought and consideration is put into this and best practice would be that children are not put to sleep in prams and pushchairs, but in well designed beds or cots or safely on covered mattresses with soft cushions.

The sensory/exploration space
(with room to crawl!)

This type of space needs to have a 'wow factor' of its own and one that reflects its purpose. Ideas might include using shiny resources, natural materials or black and white items or other contrasting coloured items that allow children to explore and investigate using all of their senses over a long period of time. Very young children use their hands and feet as well as their mouths, noses, ears and whole bodies to explore objects and materials so in this area sensory experiences need to include sensory experiences such as 'play with jelly' or collections of everyday objects to stimulate the different senses through such things as the use of treasure baskets (see *The Little Book of Treasure Baskets*: Featherstone Education).

Babies will look, listen, touch, suck, lick, bang, pick up, and drop objects thus helping them to make connections in their brains. This type of activity often encourages babies to concentrate for longer periods as they are choosing which objects to explore for themselves. Sensory play experiences will not, of course, be limited to a sensory play area of the room. That's not how the world works for a baby! However much you might think you would like to tell them not to touch, taste etc, you can save your words – it's just the natural thing to do! However, you can create a zone which is highly stimulating and builds on their natural instincts and therefore will help them create their understandings in a semi-structured way.

Money to spend?
If you have a budget, or can prioritise for spending in this area, there are some key pieces which will transform the sensory area, capture the children's attention and fuel their imaginations.

Some ideas to consider

- **projectors** can be sourced quite cheaply now and different themed slides can be projected onto walls, ceilings or light-coloured fabrics

- **bubble tubes** – balls, plastic fish can be additional visual aids within these

- **CD Player** with a variety of music can then be played to alter the mood and affect the senses

Minimum/limited funds to spend?

If you don't have enough of a budget right away, there are still plenty of ways to create a space immediately using a minimum amount of money, your imagination, donations and the skilful knowledge of how young children play and develop!

Some ideas to consider

◆ **Varying the space**
Cubby holes, corners, semi-structured dens are all good sensory play areas. More often than not, enclosed spaces are seen as ideal. These areas certainly add a contrast as 'darkness' can be created, but it is also important to consider the young age of the children, the visibility of the children within the space (if they choose to use it independently without an adult present) and also some of the youngest children's apprehensions about darkness. Creating a sensory place can be achieved just as well in an open manner; on view within the room, but in a specifically defined area of its own.

◆ **The flooring and walls**
mats: hessian, large flat cushions, reflective surfaces, black and white squares all add to the sensory experience in different ways.
cushions: different textures, patterns and prints, a variety of shapes and sizes.
drapes: hang across the ceiling, down the wall, to create a translucent divider.
mirrors: on the wall (at child's height), dangling from the ceiling to catch the light, different sizes and shapes arranged in patterns on the wall, safety mirrors on the floor give a different view and perspective of the world and themselves.
pull up bars: fixed to the wall with mirrors behind

◆ **Lighting**
Consider dimmer switches, fairy lights, coloured bulbs and coloured changing lamps.

◆ **The sense of smell**
flowers and plants (including herbs which can be living in pots or dried in cushions and linen bags).
oil diffusers, room sprays, pot pourri, dried fruit
A word of caution! Check whether any children have specific allergies or asthma, as certain aromas can cause reactions.

◆ **Creating sound**
Of course there are a variety of sounds on CDs – the sound of the ocean, the rainforest, bird song etc. but sound can be created in different ways too:
bells and chimes (perhaps strung from ribbons up high)
rustling materials and fabrics
wooden objects
water fountains (table top ones, above child-height)
clocks ticking and chiming

◆ **Themes**
The theme of your area can be changed quite easily and frequently. Remember to think openly – don't rely on traditional 'child-like' themes. Learning about the world is wider than just learning about colour. Be more creative! Some ideas to consider:

• **Shiny and glittery**	• **Natural materials**	• **Rainbows**
• **Smooth and rough**	• **Dark and light**	• **Loud and quiet**
• **Black and white**	• **Reflection and mirrors**	• **Tunnels/tubes**

The messy play space

In this area babies can use their senses to engage in messy play with a range of resources. Resources that can be used to support sensory messy play include:

- gloop
- jelly
- cooked spaghetti
- cooked pasta
- clean shredded paper

Some ideas to consider

Babies will get really messy and we need to be on hand to ensure they play in full safety. Parents will be able to tell you about any known allergies their child may have. Almost any suitable food can be used for messy play e.g beans, cornflower mixed with water, home made soft dough.

The cosy/soft play space

This area provides a space where babies can lie/sit comfortably away from the hustle and bustle of the rest of the room and watch what's going on. They may cuddle up with their key person or other children as they get older.

Some ideas to consider

Remember to keep any washable coverings clean. Provide cushions and soft throws and consider providing baby baskets where babies can sit safely unaided.

The eating space

This is a regularly used space where babies can sit and be fed by their key person – somewhere they are used to and are comfortable.

Some ideas to consider

It is important that the key person wherever possible feeds the baby/ies to whom they are the key person. Babies should where appropriate/necessary be safely fastened in to their seats. Soft and soothing background music will help to create a calm atmosphere.

The book/story space

In this area children can discover and share books, independently and with adults. For the youngest children, this area is all about developing a love of books, stories, language and rhyme. It's an exploration area like any other.

Some ideas to consider

When planning the book/story area, think carefully about the ages of the children and resource appropriately. Remember the babies will put everything into their mouths – it's just natural – and some books are designed with this in mind.

Some baby room essentials

Each baby room amongst other things needs:

- at least two adult sized comfortable chairs or a large settee so that a staff member and a parent can sit down, child on knee and talk in comfort.

- an additional chair provided which is suitably comfortable for an adult holding or comforting or feeding a child

- small pieces of furniture such as child-sized sofas or attractive low level storage units that can be used to partition/divide off areas

- pull up bar with large non-shatter mirrors behind

- drapes and soft furnishings that make it cosy and give warmth

- a stage appropriate range of toys and resources

- larger pieces of furniture placed where your eye is not drawn to them immediately on entering the room, such as by the edging walls of the room (especially importuned in smaller rooms).

Some ideas to consider

Overall the idea should be that the room gives the appearance of space with cosy corners. An effective baby room combines a sense of spaciousness with that of cosiness and intimacy. It offers a space that allows free movement for the more mobile babies and provides a quieter cosy area for babies not yet able to move much by themselves. Baby rooms should not be dominated by cots. One solution is to have fewer cots and use suitably covered mattresses in a corner of the room where babies can be sensitively placed to sleep (or place themselves) when they are tired. Whoever is supervising/monitoring that part of the room can sit close by on a low comfortable chair or on a large cushion on the floor, so placed that he/she can protect the space from intrusion by older, more mobile children, whilst still being available to interact and talk with babies as they play close by. Overall, the general layout of the room should give the maximum range of development opportunities as babies progress from crawling through to taking their first steps.

Suitable sized, covered mattresses, or cosy covered baskets, are good for babies who are at the stage of sitting propped up by cushions and those who are starting to be able to roll themselves over or levering themselves upwards. However, as soon as they begin to crawl they need the firm surface of a floor covering such as carpet, large rugs or wipe clean soft surfacing.

One key question that can be usefully asked is *'Would I be happy for my own child to attend the setting?'* If so, why? And if not, then why not? My experience is that it is all too easy for staff, in some settings, to get used to a chaotic and uncared for room environment. Without them being aware of this, it can have an unsettling effect on the staff and the children, not to mention the poor quality messages it gives to any parents/carers and visitors.

Adequate well planned storage

This is equally important in the baby room as in any other room. Key points to be discussed by the baby room leader with the staff team should include:

- definition of the roles/responsibilities of room staff

- how resources are accessibly stored

- the purpose/effectiveness of displays and hangings

- how attractive and stimulating the room is for the babies

In the toddler room

Subject to the needs of the children, number of children and suitability of the space (including access to the outdoor space) this can be two adjacent rooms – one for toddlers from 12 months to under 2 and one for children aged 2-3 or a joined up room for children aged 12 months – 3 years; but remember it's about stages not ages and some children will outgrow a room more quickly than others.

Take a good look around your space without any children in it and when a session is running. Remember the best way to evaluate space for infants and toddlers is to get down to their level. Try to see the environment from the infant's point of view. Infants spend a lot of time on the floor, so it's important that the floor is clean and comfortable. View the ceiling and walls from this perspective. What do you see? Overhead lighting can often be harsh, every available wall surface covered in 'educational' posters and the shelves at the children's level over-filled with toys.

Infants and toddlers are highly sensitive to their surroundings. While they notice everything, they cannot necessarily make good use of everything they see. It can be difficult to make a choice when there is too much to choose from. The overall aim is to create a simple and neutral backdrop and wall space, that is not overcrowded. Not only is this more restful but it allows for items and play objects to stand out. Make use of available space at children's level for child activity. Build in learning opportunities, using the walls, shelving and furniture, to place items within children's easy reach. Infants and toddlers are beginning to learn the properties of objects and materials. They develop a familiarity with soft things, hard things, heavy things, things that make a noise, and so on. Older, more mobile infants are ready to explore their surroundings more actively. Climbing, jumping and running are important activities for toddlers as they learn control of their bodies. Keep the middle of the room as an active zone to provide opportunities for infants to practise these skills. Improvise and create a multi-level environment that invites movement. Use mattresses, boxes, couches, pillow mountains, covered tyres, steps and platforms. Enhancing the provision on a regular basis provides variety and new challenges.

Keeping the environment simple encourages children to find something of interest and become actively involved in play and exploration. A well-planned environment will empower children to make their own choices and support the holistic nature of their learning. It will also provide a setting that supports the development of social relationships with peers, and the adults who care for them.

Some toddler room essentials

Each toddler room amongst other things needs:

- **a large settee so that a staff member and a parent can sit down, child on knee, and talk in comfort.**

- **an additional chair which is suitably comfortable for an adult holding or comforting a child.**

- **small pieces of furniture such as child-sized sofas and attractive low level storage units can be used to partition/divide off areas.**

- **drapes and soft furnishings that make it cosy and give warmth.**

- **a stage appropriate range of toys and resources.**

Reflecting on practice

Reflecting on practice is a crucial element of effective provision and is much encouraged by the renewed EYFS framework. It will help to develop the quality of the provision and the experiences that are offered to the children. The following are examples of the type of questions you may raise to support your self-reflection:

Does the environment appear appropriately welcoming for the children? How do you know this?

Are there some mirrors at a suitable child height for the children to see themselves in and so develop a sense of self esteem?

How often and how effectively do adults interact with children?

How do you model using new resources?

How do children use the resources on offer in the area?

Can the children easily access all aspects of the continuous provision?

How do you communicate and share ideas with parents/carers?

How do you observe children and then use these observations to enhance the environment?

How is the environment appropriately defined and maintained?

Do displays reflect the learning environment offered and also reflect the process of the learning taking place?

Are the learning spaces well defined?

Are there a number of places for the child to choose to be alone or with a friend?

Does the environment appropriately reflect cultural diversity?

It cannot be over emphasised how important it is to ensure that you regularly evaluate the spaces you provide. Consider the needs of all the children in the environment. Create changes in the environment gradually, and introduce new materials or develop new spaces over time, and observe the children's response. Even familiar materials presented in new and simple ways can be appealing to young children. Remember that play items do travel in the hands of toddlers, but providing clear, visible boundaries reminds children of where things belong. A quality environment for toddlers will include some or all of the following learning spaces subject to the size and nature of the space:

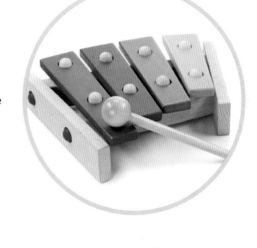

- Messy space

- Water play space

- Sand play space

- Creative play space

- Book/story space

- Domestic role-play space

- Sensory space

- Music space

- Mark making space

- Quiet/cosy space

- Soft play space

- Imaginary space for small world and construction play

Generic key features to establish in developed 'learning spaces' in the toddler rooms are:

- resources which are interesting, open ended and stored appropriately

- a safe and secure environment. This includes ensuring appropriate room temperatures, ventilation, boundaries, natural light and displaying photographs of children engaged in activities

- stimulating resources that cater for all of the senses

- a quiet, comfortable and safe environment to sleep and rest away from the hustle and bustle

- appropriately sized furniture which is safe for them to access and use

- a variety of surfaces for activities which are a balance of table top and floor based

- easy access to the outdoor learning environment

- provision enhanced on an ongoing basis according to children's identified developmental needs and interests – provision that supports all seven primary and specific areas of learning and development – continuous indoor/outdoor access

In the infant/pre-school room

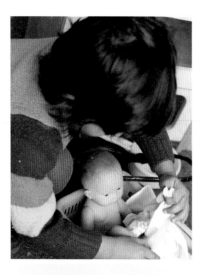

As children grow so do their skills, knowledge and interests. As with baby and toddler rooms, we must try to make the pre-school space as attractive as possible and counter any institutional/impersonal feel to the environment. There are many ways to address this, one of which is to try to include features of the home settings of the children. You can take steps to personalise and 'cosy up' the environment with the addition of:

- **family photos belonging to children**

- **objects of interest**

- **treasured items from their world**

Create a rich environment using colours, pillows, rugs, pot plants, curtains, and interesting but safe 'knick-knacks'. To add aural and visual interest, include mirrors, wind chimes, displays of natural materials, and a few well-placed mobiles. Include adult-sized furniture and child-sized furniture in the room.

A settee can provide a physical challenge for children, a great space to climb up to read a book, have a cuddle or have some time out. It's important for adults to be comfortable and available to spend time with children. By including sturdy appropriately sized furniture, we provide children with a sense of belonging – the sense that 'this is a space for me'.

Try where possible to Include:

- **plants**
- **art prints**
- **lamps for localised lighting**
- **art objects**
- **natural items**
- **flowers**
- **fabrics**

Spaces to develop in the infant/pre-school room should include **some or all** of the following subject to the nature/size of the available space and the needs of the children:

Sand area

In this space children can develop their skills in finding out and doing things with sand. The sand will sometimes be wet and at other times dry. They can engage in things like pouring dry sand, making sand castles with wet sand or using small world resources to create their own story based activities.

Water area

In this area children can develop their skills in investigating water. Water can be poured from one container into another. The water can be warm or cold, it can be coloured or a smell added to enhance its desirability/attractiveness to the children. It can be used to play out familiar stories like 'Mr Gumpy's Outing'.

Small world/Construction area

In this area children can engage imaginatively in familiar small world situations such as a farm, a garage, a roadway, a zoo, etc. using small world character/people/resources including play mats. They can build and construct with a range of construction sets and also with a wide range of found/recycled materials such as different sized boxes, tubes and containers – sometimes using tape and other joining materials.

Role-play area

In this space children can engage in domestic role-play and as they become older this can be developed to provide a familiar role-play situation such as a cafe or a shop.

Investigation/Exploration area or Messy/Sensory area

In this space children support their sensory skills with a wide range of natural and messy resources. They can explore different textures such as jelly, cornflower, gloop, beans, shredded paper, spaghetti etc. They can also, at times, explore and investigate natural materials and living things, using their senses and simple scientific tools such as magnifying glasses and simple microscopes.

Writing/Mark making/Drawing area

This provides a range of opportunities for children to use mark making resources to create marks and patterns using a range of mark making mediums. They can develop their drawing and writing skills, by creating simple messages, signs, cards or books and also create marks and patterns using a range of mark making mediums including charcoal, pencils, felt tips pens, etc.

Story/Listening area

In this space children can discover and share books or play with puppets to recreate stories themselves. They can listen to familiar taped stories, songs and rhymes and follow these in the books provided.

Creative area

In this area children can express themselves with different creative media such as paints, crayons, chalks, felt pens. They can paint, create, draw and mark make in lots of different ways using a variety of tools and materials.

ICT area

This area will host any computer/s and will also be where other resources such as remote control cars, Bee-bot mini robots and associated resources etc. are stored.

Soft play area

This provides an indoor area for children to let off steam and develop gross motor and other skills and can be particularly useful when the outdoor weather is not as suitable as it might be for gross motor physical play. This space can easily be shared across two or more rooms.

Sensory space (Heuristic play)

This offers tactile experiences with a range of objects that feel different and in some cases make a sound. It encourages the use and development of exploration skills through the senses.

Music space

This allows children to play freely with a range of percussion and other instruments. The children are supported to discover different musical instruments and learn to differentiate sounds and develop rhyme and rhythm. Music CDs which can be played allow children to move or dance to familiar background sounds or songs. It may also incorporate a small low level stage for performances of songs or rhymes.

Mirrors space

This provides a range of mirrors along with large laminated images of children in the room at child height for children to see themselves and others and so build up self confidence and self esteem.

Quiet/Cosy Space

This provides a place where children can sit comfortably away from the hustle and bustle of the rest of the room, and watch and share quietly with their favourite doll or teddy or other children... or simply rest or sleep.

Flooring

It is recommended that non-slip flooring be used and attractive, comfortable, easy to clean rugs. The once traditional wall-to-wall carpets are now best avoided, as often they need to be cleaned with strong cleaning agents. Healthy materials to use for flooring include hardwood, cork, tile or linoleum. Vinyl composition tiles (once the norm) are not really appropriate these days, as they require toxic glue and toxic chemicals for ongoing maintenance and can have a high maintenance element. Soft floor coverings such as throw rugs and blankets, should where possible be made of natural fibres such as cotton, hemp and wool.

Self evaluation

Reflecting on practice is a crucial element of effective provision and is much encouraged by the renewed EYFS framework (DfE 2012). It will help practitioners to develop the quality of provision and the experiences that are offered to the children. Similar self reflection questions to the ones considered for the toddler room (see page 27) can be used for the infant/preschool room as well as: Do displays reflect the learning environment offered and also reflect the process of the learning taking place? How do you ensure the environment supports early literacy skills and hosts a good range of speaking, listening, reading and writing opportunities? Are there appropriate interactive displays in place that engage children and support learning outcomes?

Generic characteristics of the Infant/Pre-School room

Many of the generic characteristics will be the same as for the toddler room. The environment should be planned and organised into clearly defined areas to accommodate different types/ranges of activities appropriate to the development and abilities of the children attending. Careful thought should be given to how the areas are divided. Often this will be through the use of low level shelving that reduces distraction and allows children to become engrossed in their activities. At other times it may be through freestanding dividers, plants and drapes. Low level shelving allows resources and equipment to be displayed accessibly so that children are enable to make deliberate choices about what they want to use.

A focus on essential and desirable resources

In order to support staff in setting up and developing the workshop areas described, potential resources are suggested on the following pages for each area and grouped under 'essential', 'desirable' and 'other items which can be used'. The role of staff in setting up and developing these areas is to make sure they include resources and equipment which will support children's identified interests and required learning outcomes. These will require appropriate storage so as to be attractive and accessible to children and as easy as possible for them to tidy away at the end of sessions. The general advice we would offer is to include all or most of the 'essential' resources and as many as possible of the 'desirable' ones and possibly some of the others.

Resource ideas for an infant/pre-school room

The sand area

Recommended resources

Essential	Desirable
Appropriately sized sand tray with play sand – offered in dry, damp or wet condition	Hand-held metal detector
Buckets and spades	Bark pieces, twigs and leaves
Variety of sand moulds	Driftwood
Shells, pebbles and stones	Small wooden planks (to straddle width of water tray)
Play people	Spoons of varying sizes
Trowels and rakes	Brushes
Sand wheel (dry sand)	Small cardboard boxes
Sieves and colanders	Plastic containers with lids
Small world wild animals	Plastic bottles and open containers some with holes for dry sand play
Cars and trucks	Large alphabet letters
Relevant non-fiction and fiction books related to sand play/current theme	A4 sized laminated images of children using the area
Dust pan, brush and broom	
Small world dinosaurs	

Other items that can be used in a sand area

- Small pulleys and cranes

- Fossils made by pressing things in plasticine/clay

- Real bones or bones made from plastic or baked dough

- Materials/liquids to add to sand such as

  - water
  - perfumed oils
  - paint
  - glue
  - food colouring
  - glitter
  - sawdust
  - salt
  - beads

- Tools to get things out/filter such as

  - tweezers
  - colanders
  - netting
  - tea strainers
  - chop sticks
  - holey spoons
  - tongs
  - magnets

- Plastic mirrors/mirror boards

- Mini trees and fences

- Giant dried lotus flower heads

- Recycled small containers of different sizes

- Small world-dumpers and tippers

- Chop sticks

The water area

Recommended resources

Essential
Appropriately sized water tray for the space and children's needs
Waterproof aprons
Funnels and pipes
Sponges
Water wheels
Cups and teapot for domestic play
Plastic fish and other sea creatures
Mop and bucket (to clean up excess water on floor)
Small boats
Play people
Sieves
Set of different sized jugs
Variety of small world animals
Holed containers (can be home made)
Corks, conkers and pine cones
Variety of washable dolls from different cultures

Desirable
Water tray with overhead frame to hang things from e.g. holed containers
Shells
Ping pong (or small sized plastic balls) with letters and numbers marked on them
Under-tray mat or large towels to absorb excess water
Books and posters on water/water play
Mini fishing netts
Range of plastic bottles and screw on tops
Small wooden planks (to straddle width of water tray)
Whisks
Food colouring and flavouring
Jumbo straws
Numbered ducks
A4 sized laminated photos of children using the area

Other items that can be used in a water area

- Materials to enhance water experiences including:

  - food colouring
  - mud
  - flour
  - glue
  - jelly crystals
  - soap flakes
  - sand
  - sugar
  - cellulose paste
  - salt
  - pasta
  - clay
  - florists gel crystals
  - tissue paper
  - crêpe paper
  - glitter
  - sequins
  - play jewels

- Tea strainers, holey spoons and tongs

- Bath rack to hold things

- Baby bath

- Range of different sized bowls

- Brushes and cloths

- Shells

- Pebbles

- Small fishing rods

- Spoons, scoops and cups

- Set of sized measuring flutes

- Ice cubes, frozen water in plastic gloves, bags and other containers

- Plastic 'icebergs' and arctic animals

- Real pond plants, soil and sand

- Cups and teapot sets for domestic play

- Items to use instead of water such as shredded paper, gloop, jelly

- Pumps and siphons

The small world and construction area

Recommended resources

Essential
Road mats, floor space/large mats for laying out markings
Train track, engines, carriages and buildings
Range/variety of cars and trucks
Aeroplanes and helicopters
Books on construction/topic linked
Small world dinosaurs
Garage with cars
Building site figures with trucks and diggers
Play tools in tool kit/box
Range of small world play farm animals and domestic animals
Variety of small world people reflecting differing life styles and cultures
Variety and range of wooden blocks and bricks
Small wooden blocks and planks
2 or 3 manufactured construction sets (e.g. Mobile, Stickle bricks, Lego, Bau Play etc.)
Duplo bricks
Cardboard boxes, tubes, string, tape and other joining materials
Tape measures and rulers
Space to leave 'work in progress' to be finished later
Space to celebrate and store finished constructions with labelled signage
Clip boards
Play tools/tool kits
Corrugated card, bubble wrap, packaging and recycled materials
Books and posters relating to construction

Desirable
Tuff spot (builder's tray)
Doll's house, furniture and people
Farm buildings
Access to materials to add to small world play e.g. sand, soil, stones, leaves and other vegetation
Small world mats e.g. roadway, airport and farm
Clip boards and/or notebooks to record
Tool belts with tape measures, pencils, mobile phones and notepads
Posters on buildings and bridges etc
Directories and catalogues from DIY stores, garden centres, tool hire and car show rooms
Mini planks
Fencing, trees and fields
Plastic builders' hard hats for children to wear
Washing line or board to hang/display/place designs, photos, plans and maps etc.
Space to display and label models
Space to leave work in progress
A5 and A4 size notebooks
Block play set
Camera to record structures
A4 size laminated photos of children using the area

Other items that can be used in a small world/construction area

- Corrugated card

- Bubble wrap

- Joining tape

- Figures dressed for their different professions

- Straws, string and card

- Small boxes range of shapes/sizes

- Wall board for children to draw their designs

- Woodwork bench, simple tools and resources such as planed, timber softwood off-cuts

- Gravel, foil and flour

- Fairytale and story characters

The domestic role-play area

Recommended resources

Essential
Open ended role-play structure (fixed or portable)
Child sized domestic equipment and appliances e.g. fridge, cooker, sink unit, storage unit and microwave
Notebooks, message books, appointment books and pens/pencils
Writing templates e.g. invoices, tickets and receipts
Story or related books/posters
Simple notices/signs e.g. open/closed, wait here
Child sized table and chairs
Domestic cutlery, crockery, pots and pans
Dolls and dolls' clothing reflecting different cultures/races

Desirable
Portable items such as iron, kettle, till and telephone
Ironing board
Range of dressing up clothes including aprons
Suitable dressing up stand (easy to access/use)
Pretend food
Message board
Towels
Oven glove/s
Cot/bed for dolls with accessories e.g. pillow, covers and blankets
Baby feeding bottles
A4 size laminated photos of children using the area

Early in the year, domestic role-play is likely to be the main focus but as children develop, two role-play areas can be provided – subject to space one domestic based and the other theme based e.g. cafe, garage, building site, hospital etc can be provided. Where there is only sufficient space for one role-play area indoors consider theming this but also providing a domestic role-play space outside.

Other items that can be used in a domestic role-play area
• **Real food**
• **Mobile phones**
• **Flower displays real and/or artificial**
• **Pets (soft toy)**
• **Pet accessories e.g. bowls, lead, collar etc.**

The investigation/exploration area

Recommended resources

Essential
Magnets and magnetic resources
Seeds and plants
Real fruit and vegetables
Magnifying glasses
Kaleidoscopes
Natural resources e.g. pine cones, pebbles, etc
Topic related books

Desirable
Minibeasts in tank or clear box
Torches
Pieces of textured materials of different types
Mirrors e.g. flat, concave and convex
Binoculars
Camera to record
Posters
A4 size laminated photos of children using the area

Other items that can be used in an investigation/exploration area
• Lightboxes
• Colour paddles
• Coloured acetate sheets

The mark making/writing/drawing area

Recommended resources

Essential
Variety of pencils and felt tip pens
Variety of paper and card
Laminated alphabet line
Variety of envelopes
Magnetic letters and boards
Post-it pads
Small exercise books
Chalks and blackboards
Writing frames e.g. class register, partly filled in celebration cards, postcards, tickets, message sheets etc.
Letter posting box

Desirable
Joining tools – stapler, hole punch
Joining resources – string, treasury tags
Children's name cards
Parcel and sticky labels
Diaries
Themed writing paper e.g. hedgehog theme
Children's display board for their writing/drawing
Stamps (pretend)
Mini rulers
A4 size laminated photos of children using the area

Other items that can be used in a mark making/writing/drawing area
• Paper crafting punch e.g. dolpin or heart
• Mini whiteboards and dry wipe pens
• Etch-a-sketch boards
• Spirograph
• Magnetic letters
• Old keyboards, ink pad and stamps
• Jumbo rubbers

The book/story/listening area

Recommended resources

Essential
Small storage baskets/boxes
Quality simple story books – age appropriate
Small range of puppets
Non-fiction/information books e.g. cars, fire-fighters, diggers, hospitals, lifecycles, weather
Books on diversity and celebrations e.g. 'I am Jewish', 'I am deaf', 'I use a wheelchair'
Listening base with headphones
CDs of stories and songs/rhymes with book
Cosy chairs and cushions

Desirable
Group made books e.g. 'The day it snowed', 'Our trip to the zoo'
Map/atlas type books
Book display/stand/cupboard
Story sacks
A4 size laminated photos of children using the area
Book posters

Other items that can be used in a book/listening area

- Device/s to record themselves telling the story
- Children's magazines

The malleable play area

Recommended resources

Essential
Play dough (ideally made by children)
Rolling pins (plain)
Shape cutters
Dough boards/mats
Shaping tools e.g. dough knife, plastic pastry cutter etc.
Aprons
Books relating to baking or recipes

Desirable
Baking tins
Natural clay
Wooden hammers
Flour
Patterned/textured rolling pins
Microwave play oven
A4 laminated photos of children using the area

Other items that can be used in a malleable area

- Fairy cake cases
- Mini baking moulds
- Different sized bowls
- Food essences
- Pie tins

The ICT area

Recommended resources

Essential
Remote control cars and devices
Bee-Bot mini robot/s
Child friendly camera

Desirable
Computer and suitable software
Bee-Bot mats/boards
A4 size laminated photos of children using the area

Other items that can be used an ICT area

- Internet educational games (need internet connection)
- Child friendly karaoke machine

The soft play area

Recommended resources

Essential
Large soft shapes
Large soft foam mats (with wipe clean surface)
Appropriately sized ball pool complete with range of balls
Comfortable adult sized chair/settee

Desirable
Wall-mounted baskets at different heights
Range/types/sizes of balls to throw into wall-mounted baskets
Music player with range of CDs
A4 size laminated photos of children using the area

Other items that can be used in a soft area
• Soft, fixed, low level wall pads
• Large, light, soft balls e.g. beach balls
• Large unbreakable mirrors fixed onto walls

The mirrors area

Recommended resources

Essential
Large wall mounted mirrors
Smaller free standing mirrors
Hand held mirrors

Desirable
Concave and convex mirrors
Torches
Child friendly camera
A4 size laminated photos of children using the area

Other items that can be used in a mirror area
• Hanging mirror boards e.g. from ceiling
• Distorting mirrors

The creative area

Recommended resources

Essential
Stage appropriate painting easel
Range of paint brushes – different thicknesses
Painting paper — different ready-cut sizes
Water and paint pots
Joining tape
Glue and glue spreaders
Suitable plain scissors
PVA Glue
Felt tips
Range of small tubes and recyled boxes (card and plastic) e.g. cereal boxes, small cake boxes, margarine tubs for model making
Aprons
Drying easel for paintings Small paint rollers

Desirable
Paint mixing palettes
Coloured paper off-cuts
Mixed card
Glue sticks
Old magazines and catalogues
Printing pads
Sponges
Work in progress space
Objects to use to print e.g. leaves and feathers
Small plain and textured paint rollers
Pencils
Display folded over signs (for children to write names)
Recycled tubs for paint use with paint rollers etc
A4 size laminated photos of children using the area

Other items that can be used in a creative area
• Round trays and golf balls/marbles/spoons (to make marbling pictures)
• Cotton wool buds
• Textured paper and card
• Images of artist's work
• Sticky shapes
• Shearing (shape) scissors

The sensory area

Recommended resources

Essential
Large lighted bubble tubes
Mirrors
Baskets
Range/variety of pieces of textured and coloured fabrics including ribbons
Variety of natural objects e.g. fir cones, shells
Range and variety of sponges
Reflective materials

Desirable
Tubes and cones
Chimes
Light up toys
Paper – crinkly crêpe, cellophane and shiny
Lighting tubes
Fragrance pots
CD player and CDs for background (soothing and relaxation type music)
A4 size laminated photos of children using the area

Other items that can be used in a sensory area

- Tassel shakers
- Chiffon scarves – see through
- Squeezy toys/balls (some that make noises)
- Balloons

The quiet cosy area

Recommended resources

Other items that can be used in a quiet/cosy area

- Material wall hangings
- Den type coverings

Essential
Comfortable large cushions
Comfortable child sized seating
Carpeted or large rug
Space dividers

Desirable
Drapes for atmosphere
Small foam mats
Subdued lighting
A4 size laminated photos of children using the area

The music area

Recommended resources

Essential

Suitable percussion instruments including drums, sleigh bells, tambourine, triangles and shakers
Basic range of music CDs
Nursery rhyme books and posters
CD player
Song and rhyme cards

Desirable

Microphones
CDs of music from other cultures
Large drum/s
Mini keyboard/s
Lengths of fabric to dance with
Musical mats
A4 size laminated photos of children using the area

Other items that can be used in a music area

- Range of instruments from other cultures
- Homemade instruments
- Images of musicians/ orchestras
- Child-sized stringed instruments
- CDs of classical music

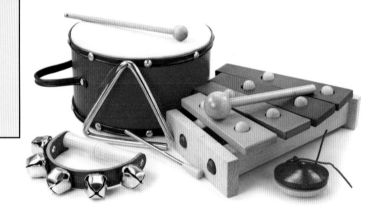

Editor's notes

This chapter will have given you many ideas to think about, discuss with colleagues and pursue, remembering that the 'essential and desirable' resource lists are there as a useful guide of what you might include and are not set in tablets of stone. The spaces and learning workshops you create will be in response to the needs and interests and cultural backgrounds of the children attending your setting and the space you have available. Not all the listed resources will be available at any one time and there will be resources not included here that are necessary/desirable for your children. This is where professional judgement comes in and where you have the opportunity to make your provision unique to meet the needs of your children.

The next chapter moves the reader on to the classroom environment in a school but the messages are the same ones that flow throughout this book. Any early years environment needs to be fit for purpose, to engage the children through establishing a 'wow factor' and to promote and offer appropriate and meaningful learning and development opportunities/experiences.

Developing workshop areas
Children in Nursery and Reception classes and EYFS units in schools

> "The learning environment significantly impacts on outcomes for children and it is therefore most important that what is provided is of a high quality and inspires children."
>
> (DfE 2011)

Much of what has already been said in the book so far is generically applicable to the environment in Nursery and Reception classes. The environment needs to be stage appropriate and to have that much needed appeal otherwise termed as the 'wow factor'. One common question is *'where and how do we make a start?'* A case study on page 81 describing an EYFS unit will help further with this but perhaps the best first step is the much tried and tested methodology of creating a design layout. This is simply a sketch plan which enables all involved to have a shared, visual concept of the proposed deployment of the existing space.

Creating a design layout

It is useful and indeed almost essential, to draw up a large outline sketch of the physical space – particularly where this is limited or very large. Then draw in where the learning spaces can best be set up, developed and used so as to maximise the opportunities for children and creating the cosy types of spaces that are needed. Overall, the key underpinning message is that it is far better to have fewer workshop areas offering more space for children than trying to cram in too many. A workshop that has insufficient space can often result in low level learning. Within all of this, due consideration needs to be given to the fact that some children may need to lie down or spread out whilst learning in some workshop areas i.e. small world. Ideally, we should try to provide as much space and as wide a variety of activities as possible but where space is limited, then some workshops will need to be combined. Some lend themselves to this more easily than others and these include:

- **The construction and small world area**

- **The book and listening area**

- **The creative and malleable area**

Before making any decision about which areas are more important you should consider the following three aspects:

- **The children's identified needs**

- **The children's recognised and predicted interests**

- **Your on-entry baseline and ongoing progress tracking data**

These three aspects will help to inform the planning of your workshop areas. For example, if your data analysis identifies creativity as a development area then priority needs to be given to workshops which support this.

The design stage

Using your knowledge of the children and your outline sketch of the floor plan then you next need to make a decision as to what to put where. This is what can be termed the 'design stage'. Once you have agreed on the position of the workshop areas, you can use the floor plan to record these. Consider using masking tape to mark out the actual size of workshop areas on the floor. This will give you a more visual idea of how things will flow and whether the spaces between areas are sufficient. When doing this you will naturally need to give due consideration to:

- **the amount of space available**
- **the location of the hard floor surface**
- **quiet areas for rest and sleep**
- **sinks**
- **fixed shelving**
- **carpeted areas**

- **natural and artificial light**
- **doorways**
- **sockets**
- **internet access points (if any)**
- **access to the outdoors**

Each of the above will dictate some aspects of the siting of each workshop area i.e. the creative workshop should be sited close to the sink and windows on hard flooring, a malleable workshop should be sited on a hard floor surface, ICT and listening areas should be sited near to the sockets. Fixed shelving lends itself to those workshop areas requiring open storage or display areas.

There will be times throughout the day/session when children will gather in larger groups for adult led group-time/circle time activities and consideration needs to be given at the design point as to where these gathering spaces will best be accommodated.

Creating/positioning gathering spaces

Consideration will now need to be given to the number of gathering spaces or key group spaces you need. It's usually best to site these in workshop areas that have the least negative impact on children's learning. The book, ICT, maths and writing areas can double up quite easily as key group spaces. It may be as simple as pushing a table or work surface quickly to one side when it's time for children to gather at group times. Once these have been agreed, they should be added to the floor plan and if appropriate marked out using masking tape.

Some areas do not lend themselves to being used for group sessions e.g. the construction area. It is worth taking time here to consider why this might be the case. A key principle of the renewed EYFS framework is that we should aim to build on prior learning and part of this is to encourage children to re-visit their learning. There is nothing more frustrating for a child, or group of children, who have invested time constructing in the block area, and who may wish to continue with their design and construction, to be told to clear it all away because it's group time. Even a basic 'tidy around' before key group would not provide adequate space for children to sit together in a construction workshop.

By now you will have almost, if not fully, created your design brief for the indoor environment. This should also indicate access point/s to the outdoor environment. In doing this you must try to be open minded and responsive and prepared to move one or two workshops around. Remember it's not always possible to achieve the perfect design brief first time. As you reflect on your design you should be thinking about how appealing it will look for the child. This should be leading you on to think of how you might divide the space in both attractive and useful ways. One way is to use space dividers.

Utilising space dividers

What do we mean by space dividers? These are simple things such as drapes, canopies, planters, single and double-sided shelving units and other items which are used to clearly define the workshop areas within the overall environment and give it that extra level of interest, cosiness and aesthetic make up. Any space dividers you use for each workshop area will need to be carefully and purposefully selected and sited, informed by children's developmental phase, their needs and also be 'fit for purpose'. By that I mean up to all the uses that children might apply to them.

A key overarching principle is to be creative with your choice of space dividers. Think of things like large planters containing two or three more exotic greenery type plants, so bringing the outdoors indoors in addition to facilitating multi-sensory learning. Children enjoy using these in their small world play e.g. dinosaurs, minibeasts etc and the stimulation of their senses adds another dimension to their learning.

Arranging furniture

Observing how your children learn in each workshop area and their development stage will inform your decisions on what furniture each workshop requires. Vary the heights of work/learning surfaces. Remember that not all workshops require a table. Children will engage in learning on unit top surfaces, the floor, low level fixed shelving and low level tables.

As a team, agree which workshops require seating and if so, what kind would be most suitable for your children i.e. cushions, chairs or a settee. As a team reflect and discuss if a workshop requires permanent seating or flexible.

If unsure move the furniture into place and see what it looks like. Try to see the space from the point of view of the child.

Ensure that you position mirrors and lightboxes and other such items at child height. Ensure children still have adequate space to learn in each workshop area once you have positioned the furniture. Ensure resources are clean, safe and in good condition.

Organising resources

The resources we present to children and the way we present them are key to high level learning. If you want your children to investigate, explore, problem solve, make connections, speculate, predict and ask questions then each resource needs to be selected with these learning behaviours and possible outcomes in mind.

Resourcing each workshop area for continuous provision i.e. the basic resources that children will require all year, so they are visible, accessible, multi-sensory, real, multi-cultural, open ended, recyclable and natural will attract and draw children into workshop areas. There needs to be a clear purpose for each resource and each one must be stage appropriate. The continuous provision for each group may be slightly different as their learning needs, interests and personalities may be different.

If the resources need to be stored in a container then try to use a variety of types in different areas e.g. wicker baskets, transparent containers, wooden and metal containers. Some resources may need shaped silhouettes on surfaces/shelving to support children's independence in returning them to a specific place e.g in the water area the measuring jugs/containers. This will also provide support for visual discrimination and maths learning.

When labelling resources you should always aim to use text and images (sometimes using more than one language if this is appropriate to children's cultural/linguistic backgrounds). Try in this and other ways to ensure a language friendly environment that facilitates independence. Consideration needs to be given to the size of font, ensuring it is stage appropriate, and the amount of text in each workshop area, as too much will simply become like 'wallpaper' and lose its effectiveness.

It is useful to have a large photographic image of each workshop area displayed so children can refer to this when they are replacing resources. See later chapters for a suggested list but remember that when resourcing areas the old adage 'less is more!' comes into play – children can have too many resources so that it becomes more counter-productive than useful.

Developing areas for literacy and numeracy

Time should be taken to identify stage appropriate literacy and numeracy learning opportunities within each workshop area. Appropriate books, interactive signs, models with signs, play dough recipes, birthday cards, photos of children learning with captions or questions, stimulus images and text will give children opportunities to develop and practise their reading, writing and numeracy skills.

Place a variety of writing materials/ supporting resources in workshop areas including:

- **writing to go box**

- **writing bag**

- **writing belt**

- **range of different sized paper**

- **range of different sized card**

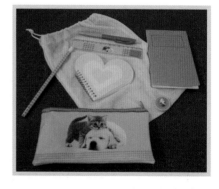

- **mini whiteboards and dry wipe felt pens**

- **clipboards**

These will appeal to a wide range of children's interests and learning styles, and give children the opportunity to engage in purposeful writing as part of their playful learning.

Playful learning

Playing alongside children in each workshop area – modelling, prompting, scaffolding and engaging children in sustained shared thinking, as well as knowing their current interests, will inform planning the next steps for each child. This information together with your observations on how children use the workshop areas, how they use the resources, what language they use, what type of play they engage in (solitary, parallel or shared), will feed into your team observation based assessment meetings. It is vital to use this observational based information to inform what resources you use to enhance the workshop areas and how the workshop areas develop.

> 'The environment is a living, changing system. More than a physical space.'
>
> (Miller J. 2007, EYFS Conference)

Try to remember Rome wasn't built in a day and the development of an environment takes time and that you will be very much at the embryonic stage early on… but that's fine both for you as practitioners and the children. As you develop the areas, take photos of children playing and learning in the workshops and share these with children in key group times. Use them to initiate discussion to move learning on. Some of these photos can be printed in A4 size, laminated and displayed in each area and others made into a book.

Maintaining workshop areas

Each workshop area requires maintaining and sustaining on a daily/weekly ongoing basis. There needs to be clear systems, consistently implemented by all staff, for replenishing workshops and final tidying and preparing – ready for the following day's or next session's learning. This of course includes ensuring resources are safe and clean. In achieving this, there is a requirement for each and every member of the team to be proactive, so the environment is an enabling one on a daily basis. Children are great copiers and will follow adults' lead. If adults value the environment, then so will children.

A multi-sensory environment

We live in a multi-sensory world and we need to reflect this in our environment. In order to grow and learn, the human brain needs to be stimulated by sensory experiences that take place in a rich and varied environment. Having a variety of plants for children to see, smell, touch and talk about provides children with multi-sensory and 'knowledge of the world' learning opportunities as well as adding to the overall aesthetic effect.

Try playing different kinds of music at an appropriate volume at varying times of the day e.g. upon entry, during free flow learning or tidying up time and observe childrens', parents' and staff responses. Placing various aromas throughout the environment e.g. large pieces of scented soap in the childrens' bathroom or entrance spaces stimulates the senses and contributes towards a positive emotional well-being. **TAKE CARE!** Make sure you check if any children have allergies to these!

We also need to think carefully about the colours used within our environment. Neutral colours such as magnolia, cream and pale buttercup on the walls and ceilings make environments appear more spacious and have a calming effect. Warm coloured accessories such as cushions and drapes give spaces an intimate, cosy feeling. Light has a significant effect on the atmosphere and mood of a room. Some children learn best in bright light whereas others learn better in low light so it is important to create both well lit and softly lit areas, enabling children to play and learn where they feel most comfortable.

The addition of fairy lights can make a space magical and inviting, drawing children into it. The use of diaphanous material as space dividers can also use light to create interesting places and facilitate investigation, exploration and stimulate children's imaginations. The lighting for each workshop area needs to be fit for purpose. Areas such as construction workshops require natural light, whereas fairy lights in the book area create a more cosy and fairy-tale mood.

Should you need to maximise natural daylight then try to place mirrors strategically around the space which will reflect and light up dark, gloomy spaces. Remember the saying that...

> 'No space is unimportant, no space is marginal. Each space communicates its own personality!'
>
> (Ceppi and Zini 1998: Aesthetic Codes in Early Childhood Classrooms)

Documenting /Defining spaces

The range of displays (interactive, instructional, informative and documenting the learning process) need to be purposeful and engage the intended audience. It is essential to have the right level of display as having too much makes the environment very busy and cluttered and having too little makes it less cosy, less attractive and defined. Both of these scenarios can have a negative effect on children's learning and behaviour.

Interactive displays may be adult-initiated but created with children or child-initiated. They should be arranged at appropriate heights and sited in ways and places fit for purpose. As young children learn through their senses there should be multi-sensory experiences on offer within these.

Each display should be clear, with an appropriate balance of resources and interactive photographs, signs and labels. Some of these may be written with the children in shared writing sessions enabling children to be familiar with the text and able to access it and understand it more easily. Displaying a good quality related book will support children's learning and adult or child-initiated writing. Interactive displays may be developed over a period of time, enabling children to build on prior learning by adding resources in response to your observations, interactions and sustained shared thinking.

Instructional displays that support children's learning such as visual timetables, photographs of children using the workshop areas effectively and prompts, may be created with children and sited at child height. Informative displays for parents/carers, students, staff and visitors should be displayed at adult height and appropriately sited e.g. EYFS staffing should be displayed by the entrance, on the parents' board in the cloakroom or by the entrance.

Documentation of children's learning requires clear, designated spaces and tools at child height for children to display their own learning. We need to respond to these displays regularly and celebrate children's achievements. Giving children the responsibility and ownership empowers them and gives the message that we value their learning.

Adult displays of children's learning should be balanced, including both the process and the end product. Documenting children's learning through a series of images and written observations of direct speech makes children's learning visible to children, parents/carers and practitioners. If a piece of work requires annotation, writing this separately on card or paper and not directly onto the child's work gives a clear message that we value their learning.

Each display serves a specific purpose and therefore needs to be used on a day to day basis with children, parents, staff and adults through modelling, sharing and referencing.

Time

> 'Children have a right to have time, give time to each other, to discuss, to explore. A time for dreaming, knowing and imagining.'
>
> An educator at a Reggio Emilia Pre-school

The whole day matters! Every minute of every day is a valuable experience. The routine of the day should ensure children have sufficient time to explore ideas and interests in depth, allowing them to become immersed in their learning. Routines should be flexible to support deep level, sustained learning and flow in response to children's needs. If we want our children to concentrate, persist, revisit and build on learning then stopping them frequently during free flow learning for direct teaching in adult focused activities will counteract this. They will become frustrated and will simply plan to learn at a more superficial level. Time should be allowed for an appropriate balance of child-initiated and adult-led experiences/activities throughout the day, time to rest, time to reflect, time to eat, time to talk and time to be listened to and time to just 'be me'.

Emotional well-being

Every child is unique! Children must have a strong sense of well-being to engage with learning. It is vital for educators to build positive relationships with parents and carers (the child's first and ongoing educators) to establish an ethos of trust and respect. As each key person welcomes and engages with parents and children at the start of the day, relationships continue to grow and flourish as they, among other things:

- **Involve parents/carers in their child's learning through home observations and ongoing access to 'learning journey'**

- **Share the day's experiences**

- **Listen and respond to parent/carer concerns or worries**

- **Communicate information and knowledge of transition systems so as to give parents and children the strong message of the value placed on the partnership working effectively.**

It is essential that strategies are put in place to support parents/carers who work and have limited contact with their child's key person e.g. through communication diaries, photographs, samples of learning through learning stories, newsletters, the daily routine (group times, phonic sessions, when they have free access to outdoors etc).

Children need time and a warm, loving relationship with their key person to ensure their well-being and help they develop a positive self-image, confidence and inner strength, independence and respect for others.

When children are in a safe, secure, trusting environment they will talk about their feelings, praise their peers, make appropriate choices, help and comfort each other and play collaboratively. They will listen to each other and talk positively about their culture and beliefs and those of others. For young children being special to someone and cared for is vital for their physical, social and emotional health and well-being. A safe secure environment with positive role models and interactions, where children are able to express their feelings helps them to build positive relationships with their peers.

The following are examples of the type of questions you may raise to support your self-reflection:

Does the environment appear appropriately welcoming for the child?

Are there mirrors at a suitable child height for the children to see themselves in and so develop a sense of self-esteem?

How do you model using new resources?

How do children use the resources on offer in the workshop areas?

Can the children easily access all aspects of the continuous provision?

How do you communicate and share ideas with parents/carers?

How do you observe children and then use these to enhance the environment?

Are there mirrors at a suitable child height for the children to see themselves in and so develop a sense of self-esteem?

How well do adults interact with children?

How is the environment appropriately defined and maintained?

Do displays reflect the learning environment offered and also reflect the process of the learning taking place?

How do you ensure the environment supports early literacy skills and hosts a good range of reading and writing opportunities?

Are there appropriate interactive displays in place that engage children and support learning outcomes?

Workshop areas to include

(space permitting and encompassing the notion that some of these areas can and may be combined)

- Sand area
- Water area
- Small world and construction area
- Role-play area
- Investigation and exploration area
- Writing/drawing area
- Book and listening area

- Malleable area
- ICT area
- Music, song and rhyme area
- Soft play area
- Creative area
- Maths/problem solving area

Resource ideas for a Nursery and Reception class

As in the previous chapter advice is provided here under the headings of essential, desirable and other items that can be used within the identified workshop areas.

The sand area

Recommended resources

Essential	Desirable
Appropriately sized sand tray with play sand – dry, damp or wet condition (staff can alternate the condition of sand)	Two sand trays – one with wet/damp sand and one with dry sand (one may be of a smaller size)
Buckets, spades	Sand tray with overhead frame to hang things from to pour water through/into e.g. holed containers
Variety of sand moulds	Driftwood
Shells, pebbles, stones,	Small wooden plank/s (to straddle width of sand tray)
Play people	Spoons of varying sizes
Trowels, rakes	Small world-dumpers and tippers
Sand wheel (dry sand)	Books on sand play
Sieves and colanders	Small cardboard boxes
Small world wild animals	Plastic containers with lids and/or plastic bottles with screw on tops
Cars and trucks	Plastic bottles and open containers some with holes for dry sand play
Relevant non-fiction and fiction books related to current theme	Hand held metal detector
Dust pan, brush and broom	Toy dinosaurs
3D wooden or plastic shapes	Blocks, bricks and tunnels for creating road ways
Holed containers (dry sand) can be homemade or bought	Bark pieces, twigs and leaves
Large alphabet letters	Small world trees/ bushes (can be fresh cuttings from local environment placed into wet sand)
	A4 sized laminated photos of children using the area
	Mini flags

Other items that can be used in a sand area

- Small pulleys and cranes

- Posters on sand/sand play cranes

- 'Fossils' made by pressing things into plasticine/clay

- Real bones or bones made from plastic, baked dough

- Water

- Small world houses

- Medium/large brush/es

- Materials/liquids to add to sand such as

  - perfumed oils
  - paint
  - glue
  - food colouring
  - glitter
  - sawdust
  - salt
  - beads

- Tools to get things out

  - tweezers
  - colanders
  - netting
  - tea strainers
  - chop sticks
  - holey spoons
  - tongs
  - magnets

- Coloured cellophane and plastic mirrors/mirror boards

- Mini trees and fences

- Giant dried lotus heads

- Washed gravel/small stones

- Recycled small containers of different sizes

- Chop sticks

- Clip boards, paper and pens for recording

The water area

Recommended resources

Essential
Appropriately sized water tray for the space and children's needs
Waterproof aprons
Range of plastic pipes for funnels
Sponges
Numbered ducks
Cups and teapot for domestic play
Fish and other sea creatures
Mop and bucket (to clean up excess water on floor)
Range of small boats
Range of play people
Sieves
Set of different sized/graded jugs
Variety of small world animals
Holed containers (can be home made)
Corks, conkers and pine cones
Variety of washable dolls from different cultures
Water wheels (large and small)
Range of spoons, scoops, pans and cups

Desirable
Water tray with overhead frame to hang things from e.g. holed containers
Shells
Pumps and syphons
Brushes and cloths
Feathers
Mini fishing nets
Range of different sized bowls
Under-tray mat to absorb excess water
Whisks
Food colouring and flavourings
Jumbo straws
Small wooden planks (to straddle width of water tray)
Mini scrubbing brushes
Range of plastic bottles and screw on tops
Set of different sized measuring flutes
Ping pong balls (or small alternative plastic balls) with letters and numbers marked on them
Books and posters on water/water play
Plastic syringes
Graded funnels
Graded cylinders
A4 size laminated photos of children using the area

Other items that can be used in a water area

- Materials to enhance water experiences including:

  - food colouring
  - mud
  - flour
  - glue
  - jelly crystals
  - soap flakes
  - sand
  - sugar
  - cellulose paste
  - salt
  - pasta
  - clay
  - florist gel crystals
  - tissue paper
  - crepe paper
  - glitter
  - sequins
  - play jewels

- Tea strainers, holey spoons and tongs

- Bath rack to hold things

- Baby bath

- Small fishing rods

- Ice cubes, frozen water in plastic gloves, bags and other containers

- Plastic 'icebergs' and arctic animals

- Real pond plants, soil and sand

- Items to use instead of water: shredded paper, gloop and jelly

The small world and construction area

Recommended resources

Essential
Road mats, floor space/large mats for laying out markings
Train track, engines, carriages and buildings
Range of cars and trucks
Aeroplanes/helicopters
Books on construction
Garage with cars
Building site figures with trucks and diggers
Range of farm animals and domestic animals
Variety of small world people reflecting different life styles and cultures
Play tools in tool kit/box
Variety and range of wooden blocks, bricks
Manufactured construction sets e.g. Mobilo, Duplo, Stickle bricks
Books relating to construction
Space to celebrate and store finished constructions with labelled signage
Space to leave 'work in progress' to be finished later

Desirable
Tuff spot (builder's tray)
Doll's house, furniture and people
Farm buildings
Access to materials to add to small world play e.g. sand, soil, stones, leaves and other vegetation
Small world mats e.g. roadway, airport, farm
Clipboards and or notebooks to record
Toy dinosaurs
Tool belts with tape measures, pencils, mobile phone and mini notepad
Smaller size construction sets e.g. Lego
Posters on buildings and bridges etc.
Mini planks
Small world fencing, trees and fields
Directories and catalogues from DIY stores, garden centres, tool hire centres and car show rooms
Notebooks and/or clipboards
Large block play set
Hard hats for children to wear
Wall board for children to draw their designs
Washing line or board to hang/display/place designs, photos, plans and maps etc.
Child-friendly camera to record structures
Large block play set
A4 size laminated photos of children using the area

Other items that can be used in a small world/construction area

- Packaging and recycled materials

- Corrugated card

- Bubble wrap

- Joining tape

- Straws, string and card

- Small planks

- Fairytale and story characters

- Small recycled boxes range of shapes/sizes

- Small block play set

- Woodwork bench with vice, simple tools and resources such as planed timber, softwood off-cuts, screwdrivers, pincers and sand paper

- Large keys calculator

- Figures dressed for their different professions with related books

- Gravel, foil and flour

- Pretend tea making resources

- Materials for rivers and grass etc.

NB: Separate small world and constructions areas can be set up but our experience is that these areas are best situated close to/next to each other or joined up as we recommend.

The domestic role-play area

Recommended resources

Essential
Open-ended role-play structure fixed or portable
Child sized domestic equipment and appliances e.g. fridge, cooker, sink unit, storage unit, microwave, cutlery, place mats and tea towels etc
Notebooks, pads, message books, appt books and pens/pencils
Writing frameworks e.g. invoices, tickets and receipts
Story or related books/posters
Simple notices/signs e.g. 'Open/Closed', 'Wait here'
Child sized table and chairs
Domestic cutlery, crockery pots and pans
Dolls from range of cultures and clothing
Doll's cot/bed
Doll's feeding bottles

Desirable
Portable items such as iron, kettle, till and house phone/mobile phones
Ironing board
Range of dressing up clothes including aprons
Suitable dressing up stand – easy to access/use
Pretend food
Message board
Baby bath and towel/s
Oven gloves
Dressing up clothes/outfits
A4 size laminated photos of children using the area
Doll's highchair

Often children will start with domestic role-play on entry to the nursery and later this will change to themed role play. Where possible, two indoor role-play areas should be set up, one domestic based and the other theme related. Where space does not allow for two indoor role-play areas then opportunities for domestic role-play should be offered outdoors.

There are many themes that can be developed through role-play including: Post office, Flower shop, Travel agents, Doctors, Hospital, Pet shop, Hairdressers, Dentists, Cinema, Café, Museum, Garden centre, Building site. Gym/Keep fit centre, Pirate's cave, Baby shop, Fruit and vegetables shop, Toy shop, Santa's grotto, Science lab, Police station etc.

Whatever is chosen should reflect children's experiences/levels of understanding and hence where possible a visit should be part of the preparation for this. Each will have their own specific resources/items related to the theme for example:

Post office: forms, stamps, signs, posting box

Flower shop: displays, artificial and/or real flowers, order pads, receipts

Pet shop: soft animals, pet accessories e.g. bowls, lead, collar, cages etc.

Travel agents: tickets, travel brochures, currency, extra trip info

Cinema: tickets, refreshments, seating plan, times of films, feedback forms.

In some situations the use of real food may be on some occasions appropriate e.g. café, cinema.

There are many books good on role-play available (see *Role Play in the Early Years, Featherstone*) and where practitioners need more detailed ideas it is recommended that one or more of these are consulted.

The writing/drawing area

Recommended resources

Essential
Variety of pencils, felt tips
Paper and card
Mini rulers
Variety/range of envelopes
Laminated alphabet line
Old unused diaries
Small exercise books
Chalks and mini chalk boards
Magnetic letters and boards
Letter posting box
Pencil sharpeners
Whiteboards and wipe dry pens
Rubbers
Place/space to display writing/drawings
Post box

Desirable
Writing frameworks e.g. celebration cards, variety of forms, invitations
Joining tools (stapler), hole punch
Joining resources: string, treasury tags
Children's name cards
Parcel and sticky labels
Sellotape and dispenser
Themed writing paper e.g. hedgehog theme
Children's display board for their writing/drawing
Stamps for letters (made)
Small class registers
Key words: stage appropriate selected laminated words (e.g. can be tricky words etc.)
A4 size laminated photos of children using the area
Phonic phase mats
Simple dictionaries (bought or made)

Other items that can be used in a writing/drawing area

- **Paper crafting punch e.g. dolphin or heart**
- **Etch-a-sketch boards**
- **Spirograph**
- **Charger type plates with coloured sand and small sticks/brushes to draw letters etc**

- **Post-it pads**
- **Old keyboards**
- **Ink pads and stamps**
- **Jumbo rubbers**

NB: The writing area can be usefully themed as a den or office etc. so as to make it more attractive to the children.

The investigation/exploration area

Recommended resources

Essential	Desirable
Magnets and magnetic resources	Minibeasts in a tank or clear box e.g. tadpoles, stick insects, spiders, giant snails etc.
Seeds and plants	Torches
Real fruit and vegetables	Pieces of textured materials of different types
Magnifying glasses	Mirrors e.g. flat, concave, convex
Kaleidoscopes	Binoculars
Natural resources e.g. pine cones, pebbles, etc	Child friendly camera to record
Relevant books	Posters
	A4 size laminated photos of children using the area

Other items that can be used in an investigation/exploration area

- Lightboxes
- Colour paddles
- Coloured acetate sheets

The book/story/listening area

Recommended resources

Essential	Desirable
Small book storage baskets/boxes	Class/group made books e.g. 'The day it snowed', 'Our trip to the zoo'
Quality simple story books (age appropriate)	Map/atlas type books
Small range of puppets	Book display stand/cupboard
Cosy chairs and cushions	Posters on books
Non-fiction/information books e.g. Cars, Fire fighters, Diggers, Hospitals, Lifecycles, Weather	Story sacks
Books on diversity and celebrations e.g. 'I am Jewish', 'I am deaf', 'I use a wheelchair'	A4 size laminated photos of children using the area
Listening base with headphones (ideally wireless headphones)	Treasure basket of resources to explore sound making i.e. shell, wooden block and stick, whisk etc.
CDs of stories and songs/rhymes with appropriate/linked book	Laptops or i-pads

Other items that can be used in a book/listening area

- Device/s to record themselves telling the story
- Children's magazines

The malleable play area

Recommended resources

Essential
Play dough (ideally made with children)
Plain rolling pins
Shape cutters
Dough boards/mats
Range and variety of shaping tools e.g. dough knife, pastry cutters etc
Aprons
Books relating to baking or recipes

Desirable
Baking tins
Natural clay
Wooden hammers
Flour
Microwave oven for pretend cooking
Textured rolling pins
A4 size laminated photos of children using the area
Birthday cake resources including number candles

Other items that can be used in a malleable area

- Cup cake cases
- Mini moulds
- Different sized bowls
- Food essences
- Pie tins

The ICT area

Recommended resources

Essential
Remote control cars
Bee-Bot mini robots
Child friendly camera
Computer
Stage appropriate quality software programmes e.g. Mouse in the House, Tizzy's First Tools, Animated Alphabet
Floor mats for Bee-Bots
Digital camera

Desirable
Remote control devices e.g. i-bug
Internet access
Perspex boards for Bee-Bots
Range of other portable items such as torches, simple voice recording devices, simple video recording devices e.g. Tuff cams
Karaoke machine
A4 size laminated photos of children using the area

Other items that can be used an ICT area

- Internet educational games *(need internet connection)*
- Talking postcards

NB: It is useful to have catalogues from those supplying ICT devices/equipment or to go on their websites as so much more is becoming available each year and you need to include new items periodically. The TTS group is a particularly useful supplier but many more are in the market place but so do search and shop around.

The soft play area
Recommended resources

Essential
Large soft shapes
Large soft foam mats (with wipe clean surface)
Appropriately sized ball pool, complete with range of balls
Comfortable adult sized chair/settee

Desirable
Wall mounted baskets (different heights)
Range/types/sizes of balls to throw into wall-mounted baskets
Music player with range of CDs
A4 size laminated photos of children using the area

Other items that can be used in a soft area
• Soft fixed low level wall pads
• Large, light, soft balls e.g. beach balls
• Large unbreakable mirrors fixed onto walls

NB: In most cases this will be sited in a room adjacent to the classroom or directly linked to it.

The music, song and rhyme area
Recommended resources

Essential
Suitable percussion instruments including drum, sleigh bells, tambourine, triangles, shakers
Range and variety of music CDs e.g. 'Sticky Kids'
Song and rhyme cards with words and pictures
Children's music and rhyme books e.g. 'Bobby Shaftoe'

Desirable
Streamer sticks
Mini sized battery operated organ
Echo microphone
Karaoke machine (from ICT area)
Dressing up clothes
Posters on music and rhyme
Large gathering drum
A4 size laminated photos of children using the area

Other items that can be used in a music, song and rhyme area
• Simple/basic web cam linked to the interactive whiteboards for children to see themselves performing
• Easy to use child friendly video recording devices (e.g. Tuff cams) to record each other
• Simple recorders but these need to be carefully managed as can spread infection

• Child sized guitars

• Simple instruments made by the children

The creative workshop area

Recommended resources

Essential
Stage appropriate painting easel
Range of painting brushes – different sizes and thicknesses
Painting paper – range of ready cut sizes
Water and paint pots
Joining tape – masking/sellotape/electrician's tape
Glue and glue spreaders
Scissors
PVA Glue
Felt tips
Small, recyled boxes and tubes card and plastic e.g. cereal boxes, small cake boxes, margarine tubs
Aprons
Drying easel for paintings
Pencils

Desirable
Paint mixing palettes
Coloured paper off-cuts and other items suitable for collage (e.g. shiny sweet wrapping paper)
Mixed card
Glue sticks
Old magazines and catalogues
Printing pads
Sponges
Work in progress space to leave created objects to dry
Objects to use to print e.g. leaves and feathers
Small plain and textured paint rollers
Ready made display signs (folded over) for children to write names)
A4 size laminated photos of children using the area
Ribbon, string and wool
Feathers

Other items that can be used in a creative area
• Round trays and golf balls/marbles/ spoons (for marbling activities)
• Cotton wool buds
• Textured paper and card
• Images of artist's work
• Sticky shapes
• Old buttons and other materials and fabrics for collage

The maths/problem solving area

Recommended resources

Essential
Suitable age appropriate jigsaws
Variety of puzzles and games
Open ended items to sort and match
Laminated large number line
Number based books
Measuring tapes and rulers
Variety of dice

Desirable
Calculators
Large numbers (wooden or plastic)
Magnetic numbers and mini boards
3D shapes – small coloured blocks
Sorting tray
Simple scales
A4 size laminated photos of children using the area

Other items that can be used in a maths/ problem area
• **Number washing line**
• **Variety of number lines, sticks and squares**
• **Number fans**
• **Number game**
• **Shape construction e.g. Polydron**

Editor's notes

Having read this chapter you should be fired up and ready to begin to plan your classroom or to review and update some aspects of it.

Remember that all classrooms are unique and all spaces will offer different challenges to creating an indoor environment that will inspire your children. These essential, desirable and other possible resources are presented as a guide to support your development and it is unlikely that all of these would/should be included at any one time.

That much mentioned 'less is more' guideline springs to mind again on this point. If your classroom is particularly small and if you are in a Reception class you could consider using some of the corridor space for quieter types of areas e.g. The Book/Listening Area but only if this is seen as suitable and safe. You will need to watch the children using the areas/resources you have set up and provided and then make any necessary adjustments on the basis of what you observe.

Overarching advice

Not all of these resources will be in any area at any one time and those provided will be subject to the assessed needs and interests of the children and in some cases will be topic/theme linked. Resources should be easily accessible and should, as appropriate, reflect different cultures and needs e.g. play people in wheelchairs, asian/black families, etc.

Chapter 5

Developing a workshop based approach in Year 1

> "As children get older they still learn best in the same active, hands on ways using their senses. So why should we change our approach so radically when they move into year 1 and beyond?"
>
> Terry Gould (2008)

When children move into Year 1 they often have difficulties in making the adjustment to their new environment, particularly where it merely comprises table and chairs. Most children during the preceding one, or two years will have been learning through child-initiated play, independent active learning and adult-led learning in a rich early years environment. The government funded, research based guidance 'Continuing The Learning Journey' (DfE 2008) recognised the need to make some changes to traditional Year 1 classrooms to support the transition process by providing continuity of environment and practice. This will enable those children who have not yet met the established development norms of achievement to do so in a more supportive environment than the traditional Year 1 classroom.

Some schools set up an environment in Year 1, reflecting the EYFS, only until the end of the Autumn Term when they revert to the very formal classroom. My experience has shown me that this is somewhat short sighted as children need longer than this. Indeed, some schools have now established workshop style environments in Year 2 classes as well as Year 1 having discovered the improved outcomes this produces. Additionally, there are other schools who have adopted the workshop based approach throughout the school right through to Year 6 and have achieved outstanding outcomes from Ofsted inspections. I personally have experience of working very effectively in a Year 4 class with some workshop based activities on offer and outcomes were very high indeed. I do recommend that schools should at least have a role-play area set up in every classroom and this is the starting point for many to experience the benefits.

When Year 1 classrooms adopt the workshop style approach it's very much down to how the adults and the children use the environment. Whereas in the most effective Reception classrooms (EPPE 2006) there is balance of around 50/50 between adult led/directed tasks and child self-initiated learning, in Year 1 this will change and children will be more directed at times to undertake specific independent tasks in these areas e.g. 'listen to the story in the listening/book area and then draw your favourite character and write a sentence about them'. My experience is that successful Year 1 classes who adopt the approach identified in this chapter will establish a balance of around 70/30 between adult led/directed tasks and child-initiated ones which by the end of the year will have perhaps moved to an 80/20 balance.

Reflecting on practice, how it is working and what the children are getting from their experiences is a crucial element of ensuring that effective provision is in place as it will help practitioners to further develop the quality of the provision and the experiences that are offered to the children. Practitioners (teachers and TAs) in Year 1 will need to reflect on how engaged the children are with their learning and what the outcomes are from the way the classroom operates. This will naturally include how it supports the key areas of Literacy and Numeracy as well other curriculum areas.

The following are examples of the type of questions Year 1 staff may raise to support their self-reflection:

How does the Year 1 environment and routine work for the children?

How do we communicate and share ideas with parents/carers to help them understand what we are doing is for the benefit of their child?

How do we find the time to observe children in activities in the developed areas and then use this to enhance the environment and plan for future learning through identifying the next steps?

How is the environment appropriately defined and maintained?

Do our displays reflect the learning environment offered and also reflect the process of the learning that is taking place?

How do we ensure the environment really does support early literacy skills and hosts a good range of reading and writing opportunities?

The following seven workshop style areas (including the teaching space) are those which successful Year 1 classes have included and developed and which have been proven to work well. They are, as I see it, manageable but you may wish to include one or two more – that's your choice but you would not want to include less! You will see that within the suggested areas there is a strong emphasis on those areas which particularly support literacy and numeracy.

We have to remember that this is not EYFS and that it is unlikely we will be able to include all the EYFS areas in our Year 1 classrooms. Having said that, I have worked with two schools where they wanted to do this and did include all the areas from the EYFS. One had a huge classroom and the space and funding to do so. The other was a double form entry school who knocked part of the wall down between the two classes and made it into a Year 1 unit, with the areas set up across both classrooms. I have to say things worked really well in both these schools and I put a lot of this down to very enthusiastic staff who wanted it to happen because they believed it was the best approach for their children. Both also achieved well at their following Ofsted inspections with outcomes of good or better.

These are the minimum recommended areas:

1 **The role-play area**

In this area children will engage in familiar role-play situations such as a post office, an airport, a café, a garden centre, a vets or a food shop. There will be a strong focus on the range of language and literacy development opportunities provided within this area.

2 **The writing/drawing area**

This area will provide children with a wide range of interesting opportunities for them to write and draw. It will include resources to help develop writing skills, to create simple messages, signs, cards or books etc using a range of mark making mediums such as charcoal, pencils, felt tips, pens, etc.

3 **Reading/listening area**

In this area children can discover and share books or play with puppets to recreate stories themselves. They can listen to familiar taped stories, songs and rhymes and follow these in the books provided. This area will house class made books as well as books about diversity, quality storybooks, non fiction books etc.

4 **Messy/creative workshop**

This area will provide a wide range of opportunities for children to create using their skills, knowledge and imagination. The area's resources and activities can be varied week on week as required by the needs of the curriculum and children's interests.

Children can develop their skills in finding out and doing things with sand. The sand will sometimes be wet and at other times dry. They can engage in things like pouring dry sand, making sandcastles with wet sand or using small world resources to create their own story based activities.

Children can develop their skills in finding out and doing things with water. Water can be poured from one container into another. The water can be warm or cold, it can be coloured or a smell added to enhance its desirability/attractiveness to the children. They can play out familiar stores like Mr Gumpy's Outing. It will basically be a step up/higher expectations from the Reception year.

5 Maths investigation and construction area

This area will be a place to store and use maths resources and other associated problem solving activities including jigsaws, puzzles, peg boards, pattern making boards and resources, maths board games, laces, beads and other threading resources. They can, in this area, build and construct imaginatively with a range of construction sets and also with a wide range of found/recycled materials such as different sized boxes, tubes and containers, sometimes using tape and other joining materials/resources. As it will be mainly floor space, with perhaps a table, ICT devices such as programmable cars or Bee-Bots mini robots can be used in this area.

6 ICT area

This area will host any classroom computer/s (ideally a minimum of three or more) and will also be where other resources such as remote control cars, Bee-Bot mini robots and associated ICT resources are stored.

7 Teaching area/space

This will have tables and chairs for up to 12 children and can be used for a variety of direct teaching purposes e.g. guided reading/writing. Often this will be sited within a central space within the room.

Within two of these spaces will be located gathering spaces for group/circle time. One could best be sited within the Reading/Listening area and the other the Maths Investigation/Construction area as these areas would lend themselves more easily to having the floor space to accommodate this.

The above workshop areas should have that same sort of feel and appeal that those in Nursery/Reception have and will include many of the same/similar resources but with some additions. The biggest change will be the higher expectation as to their use for children whose knowledge, skills and understanding are growing at a fast rate. There will be some additional resources added relating to the Year 1 curriculum and these can be identified by the school over time.

Children will already have developed independence skills and should be able to access an outdoor area for some activities which cannot be provided daily indoors or on the scale required . This may well include outdoor maths games or water play etc. Staff who are not EYFS trained or have no experience of the way the EYFS works will need to engage with EYFS staff in the school and carefully read earlier chapters in this book so as to gain the flavour/ethos of what is being advised. This will apply to resources for the areas and Year 1 staff should use those advised for Nursery/Reception classes as a guide to select from and add to, bearing in mind the needs of the children and the Year 1 curriculum on offer.

Considerations as to where to site these areas will be determined by the size and nature of the space available. Often when I advise on Year 1 environments, we start by drawing an outline sketch and then mark it on the floor using masking tape. This allows for an overview and sometimes leads to minor changes e.g. size of a specific area such as the role-play area. You will need to think about the following:

- **Identification of ways existing furniture can be used and the requirements for new furniture to store and set up/divide the areas**

- **Reflection on floor coverings existing and future possible**

Often traditional Year 1 classes are already set up as all carpet or mainly carpet with perhaps a small area of wipe clean floor surface. One key aspect is to ensure that how they will be used is clear for any staff and the senior leadership team of the school. This will mean that a routine of the day will need to be established for each day of the week. Initially it is best to fill in what times each day the class is already committed to/ timetabled for e.g. assembly, PE, morning/afternoon play, phonics, lunch etc. (see sample timetable below). This will clarify what is left to use and it can then be thought through how it will be used to support learning whether it be:

- **adult-directed activity**

- **adult-focused teaching**

- **children's free choice activity**

This can and will vary from school to school and half tern to half term and therefore a completed sheet for the daily/ weekly routine would not be helpful but it should consider things such as :

- **guided reading**

- **guided writing**

- **the full breadth of curriculum plans for the half term**

- **individual/groups of children's next steps**

- **individual/groups of children's interests and needs**

- **Any SEN individual programmes**

> **Tip**
>
> **On floor coverings I always say use what's there already but when replacing go for wipe-clean surfaces as suggested in previous chapters, with moveable/washable rugs.**

Days	9.00-9.30am	9.30-10.30am	10.30-10.45am	10.45-11.15am	11.15-12 noon	12-1pm	1-2pm	2-2.15pm	2.15-3.00pm	3.00pm
Monday	Assembly		Morning play	Phonics		Lunch		Afternoon play		Home
Tuesday	Assembly		Morning play	Phonics		Lunch		Afternoon play		Home
Wednesday			Morning play	Phonics		Lunch		Afternoon play		Home
Thursday			Morning play	Phonics		Lunch		Afternoon play		Home
Friday	Assembly (alt)		Morning play	Phonics		Lunch		Afternoon play		Home

Another consideration is how observations of children can be made within these areas, whether during adult-directed or child chosen activity. Here the role of the adult will need to be discussed and thought about. Most classes have a full time TA or for at least half of the day as well as the teacher. This would mean that either the teacher or the TA would need to identify/allocate some time for observations – perhaps using a camera and a formatted observation sheet. If this idea of observation is a new concept for some Year 1 staff (as is often the case) then the expertise of those in the EYFS should be drawn upon. A key point to be addressed will be that only significant things should be recorded and that any written observation whilst being detailed should not be too lengthy unless there is a specific reason for this.

Some of the observations that staff have fed back to me have included:

- **Children independently making a label for the model they have made**

- **Children's imaginative and social skills within the role-play area**

- **A child reading a book with a puppet in the book/listening area**

- **A child making a detailed clay model in the creative workshop**

Each observation that is made has been later linked to either the EYFS development matters/early learning goals or to the KS1 identified outcomes and the next steps for that child. This does have implications for staff having a detailed knowledge of both the EYFS and Year 1 required outcomes and understanding the potential of the workshop areas they have created.

Sometimes there is a resistance by Year 1 staff to move to this type of provision but often this is because they are worried about not being as effective within this sort of set up. My experience is that they do need some ongoing support either from within the school or from outside. This must include encouragement for their efforts and advice on how to keep moving forward. Some of the most challenging Year 1 teams I have worked with have, after a few months into this change, said they had wished they had adopted the style of working earlier!

Finally, one must not forget about the parents/carers and of course other staff and governors within the school. This new way of working must be explained to them on an ongoing basis and how it will help their children to achieve at an even higher level; by providing more continuity from their time in the EYFS and more practical hands on experiences with which they will engage.

Editor's notes

A copy of the guidance 'Continuing the Learning Journey' (DCSF) was given to all schools in 2008. This will provide some even more in depth thinking as to why we should consider working this way in Year 1 classes. At the time of writing, this was still available to download from the internet, and is to my view well worth doing. Some schools have taken the concept of more active learning on board in different ways. Some have:

- Established role-play areas in all primary classrooms in the school

- Used the Year 1 model across all primary classrooms

- Used the Year 1 model across both Year 1 and Year 2 classrooms

Using the indoor learning environment for child-initiated and adult-led activities

A focus on the role of the adult

> "In planning and guiding children's activities, practitioners must reflect on the different ways that children learn and reflect these in their practice."
>
> (DfE 2011)

The renewed Early Years guidance 2012 indicates that we must begin to plan using children's individual stages of development and their identified needs and interests and preferred learning styles. The unique child is therefore the starting point and as a practitioner, you must ensure that whatever you do is purposefully undertaken to improve outcomes in learning and development for the children in your care, including planning of those important next steps for each child. You must ensure through your practice, both individually and as a team, that you support…

children's learning and development across the prime and specific areas of learning and their progress towards the early learning goals.

In addition to this you need to plan to…

ensure that children have opportunities for purposeful play indoors (and outdoors), provide for both adult-led and child-initiated activity and show how you intend to help children to develop the characteristics of learning, which are:

- **playing and exploring - children investigate and experience things, and 'have a go'**

- **active learning – children concentrate and keep on trying if they encounter difficulties, and enjoy achievements**

and

- **creating and thinking critically –**

> "children have and develop their own ideas, make links between ideas, and develop strategies for doing things."
>
> (DfE 2012)

The lynch pin in the learning process

The learning environment that you design and create for your children is extremely important and as we have already identified can make all the difference to their feelings of security and their interest in learning.

However, it is essential to remember that it is you – the adult – that is the essential lynch pin in the process of learning. With all the discussion about creating spaces and providing resources, it is easy to underestimate the value of observant, interested and knowledgeable adults in supporting and guiding children's learning.

The role of the practitioner is a complex one, requiring a real commitment to the children in your care and the flexibility to take on a range of different responsibilities. However, it is also both a fascinating and awe-inspiring one. Every day your work with children will be different and you have, in many ways, to react to the moment and to know just which role to take at any particular time.

Key facets of the role of the adult

Practitioners should provide –

> "a secure foundation through learning and development opportunities which are planned around the needs and interests of each individual child and are assessed and reviewed regularly"
>
> "Each area of learning and development must be implemented through planned, purposeful play and through a mix of adult-led and child-initiated activity."
>
> (DfE 2012)

To provide enjoyment and a passion for learning
The way you introduce a resource, a theme or an activity can make all the difference between surface level learning and real in-depth fascination and the desire to learn more. Let yourself have fun alongside the children because they need to see that learning is an enjoyable process and that it can last throughout a lifetime. Show them your enthusiasm for finding out how something works and display your excitement at discovering a new fact or enjoying a story. Be prepared to get inside the sand pit with them and get paint on your clothes – they will feed off your enthusiasm.

To stimulate children's interest
As children develop they will naturally bring a multitude of questions to any given activity – that doesn't mean you can't ask some too! Throw in some of your own that might spark their interest in a different way. Guard against asking 'closed questions' (the ones with a very limited response e.g. 'yes' or 'no' or 'it's red'). Instead, try to ask 'real', open-ended questions where possible; ones that will lead to purposeful investigations and extended activities and conversations e.g. 'I wonder what will happen if…?' or 'How does…?' These will lead to deeper level thinking and learning.

However stimulating and attractive the learning environment is that you have set out for the children, there are always going to be certain areas that individual children return to again and again and those that they are more reluctant to engage with. This is where you come in. Sensitive intervention is the key. Demanding that a child participates in a given activity in say, the creative area, will only raise their anxieties and heighten their reluctance. Again, if you make it look exciting, set realistic challenges, link in with their interests and show an enthusiasm yourself, the chance of stimulating the child's interest is so much higher.

To transfer/share knowledge and skills

In recent years, it seems that many people are reluctant to think of their role as 'teaching' children skills and knowledge. The word 'facilitating' has become much more widely used and accepted. Have no doubt that children bring with them immense capacity to construct knowledge and meaning. It is awe-inspiring to hear the theories and rationales that they construct. But, we all have skills and knowledge to share and the role of the adult in helping young children learn is no different.

Imagine how frustrated you would be in the following situation: You are trying to use a new computer program, the screen is confusing and all the icons are in different positions from the program you are familiar with. The person next to you is proficient at using the program and is completing their tasks speedily, whilst you are struggling to get started. You ask for help, but your colleague suggests it's better that you just keep trying and experimenting for yourself. You continue for a while, watch them successfully complete their work and walk away, whilst you are still at pains to produce anything that resembles what you wanted.

For most people, this would be totally dispiriting – some may even give up trying. There is definitely a place for experimentation and finding out for yourself, but there is also a distinct place for 'teaching' – the sharing of knowledge and skills. Children need to be shown how to use a pair of scissors, they need to be shown how to tie to their shoes, hold a knife and fork etc. It's called 'scaffolding' and 'modelling' their learning and it can be a really important element!

To scaffold and model

Through playing alongside the children you can give valuable cues, hints and prompts to guide them to be able to successfully achieve a task or learn a new skill. Children actively copy those around them. This impulse to copy can be harnessed e.g. sit alongside a child and thread a pattern of beads or make a sandcastle and they will learn the skills from you. Verbalising what you are doing will make it even more effective. As the children become more proficient, you can gradually reduce the number of 'scaffolds' you give to them.

Join in and participate in child-initiated play

Just because a play and learning activity is initiated by a child or children, it doesn't give the adult carte blanche to stand back and leave the children to their learning. It takes a very skilful adult to play alongside in a sensitive and realistic manner and an even more skilful one to gauge when and how to intervene in that play.

You need to allow the children the freedom to try out their ideas, be spontaneous and follow their imaginations, whilst being willing and ready to contribute something of your own. Be aware that children are practising and refining very many things through their play; they may be working through an emotional need, they could be rehearsing a role they do not normally take (in either their home or school environment) or they may be developing a skill they have seen others use. Or they could be purely enjoying the feeling and sensation of what they are doing e.g. sand or water play. Before intervening, observe and listen carefully to make sure you are providing just what they need at that given moment in time.

To talk and interact with children

Talking to children in all the different areas of the environment and during the variety of activities on offer, introduces a wealth of vocabulary and language structures. Some of this is very subject specific e.g. the vocabulary which describes shapes and measures and the way in which traditional or fairy stories are told.

'Descriptive commentary' is a term given to the process of describing out loud what a child is doing, for example when building a tower. By engaging in conversations, you are helping them understand social interactions. They learn the rules and conventions of conversations and build the skills to initiate and respond in conversations with their peers. Enriching children's experiences with natural language opportunities is giving them firm foundations for learning now and in the future.

To structure play opportunities

This does not mean that you have to have a detailed plan of how the whole play experience will work for every minute of the day. However, alongside child-initiated play, there is, of course, a place for more structured activities. These may relate to setting up particular activities because you have observed a particular interest amongst the children e.g. a mechanics workshop for children particularly fascinated by cars. It could also be an activity designed to practise a specific skill which some children need help with e.g. a shared game of skittles may help develop turn-taking or co-ordination.

To help children to make the links in their learning

The idea of structuring the play opportunities, as well as grabbing every child-initiated learning opportunity that there is, is to help children build up their repertoire of experiences and to establish the links between each episode of learning. One of the greatest roles you can play as an adult in the indoor learning environment is to allow children the time and space to replay and refine their activities (see Time and Space audits in Chapter 6). They need time to concentrate and persevere and they need the permission to abandon tasks and then return and revisit things in a different way. By observing children carefully, it will also be possible to determine what opportunities need to be offered next to allow for the children to build up the links in their learning. For example, if a child has been experimenting with rolling and cutting play dough or clay, other tools could be brought into the area, or the rolling and cutting skills could be refined and practised further in a different but related activity, such as baking.

To adapt

Adaptation is the key. Every child is different; they have their own unique personalities, interests and learning styles. This is why flexibility in constantly re-evaluating your provision and approach, then being prepared to adapt and change it for individual children's needs, is the most important approach you can bring to working with young children. Much of the above advice on the role of the adult will be greatly supported by a quality indoor learning environment that is easily accessible to all children and supports an appropriate balance of both adult-led and child-initiated learning opportunities. There needs to be fore-thought given to children being able to access the environment with physical impairment and who perhaps require a wheelchair to be mobile.

The indoor environment is critical for finding out about children as (along with the outdoors) it provides the space and the place for effective and appropriate observation and interactions with children. Observations of children will almost always, in some way, reflect the quality of the learning environment. It is a good idea to sometimes make the focus of observation on aspects/areas of provision to reflect on how these are being used or not being used by children and then as a team to use this information to decide how improvements can be made which will impact on future outcomes.

To reflect on the provision

Reflecting on practice is a crucial element of effective provision and is much encouraged by the renewed EYFS framework (DfE 2012). It will help practitioners to develop the quality of the provision and the experiences that are offered to the children. The following are examples of the type of questions you may raise to support your self-reflections:

- **Does the environment appear appropriately welcoming for the child?**

- **Are there mirrors at a suitable child height for the children to see themselves in and so develop a sense of self-esteem?**

- **How do you model using new resources?**

How do children use the resources on offer in workshop areas?

Can the children easily access all aspects of the continuous provision?

How do you communicate and share ideas with parents/carers?

How do you observe children and then use these to enhance the environment?

How well do adults interact with children?

How is the environment appropriately defined and maintained?

Do displays reflect the learning environment offered and also reflect the process of the learning taking place?

How do you ensure the environment supports early literacy skills and hosts a good range of reading and writing opportunities?

Are there appropriate interactive displays in place that engage children and support learning outcomes?

The next chapter looks at three case studies which will again support the earlier chapters by giving an insight into some real life experiences on developing practice and provision in the early years.

Chapter 7

Case studies

The following three case studies are all based on real life situations and are provided to offer further advice and insight into developing and using the indoor learning environment in a range of settings – a primary school, a children's centre and a day nursery. The studies are aimed at further supporting the advice and ideas already provided in the previous chapters.

Case study 1 — Developing an Early Years Foundation Stage Unit

St Patrick's RC Primary School, Manchester

We began the development process at St Patrick's with a 'visioning' team meeting where we looked at images of a range of indoor learning spaces and discussed what learning we wanted our children to engage in. We all agreed we wanted the children to be independent, confident learners with time each day to initiate their own learning and time to revisit and build on that learning. We felt it was important to invest time in identifying the resources our children needed – informed by the data, their interests and their personalities.

Our indoor environment is a challenging space consisting of an extremely large open area with a very high ceiling. The environment was previously two spacious classrooms that had been knocked through and connected by a quite steep bridge, similar to a 'Three Billy Goats' bridge. Apart from two recessed cloakrooms and a recessed entrance area, there are no walls or dividers to break up the space or absorb sound.

A row of large Victorian windows run the length of the unit providing quite limited natural lighting due to the wire trellis covering half of each window and the attached veranda roof. There are sixteen fluorescent strip lights on each side of the unit.

The relatively new flooring is a mixture of carpet and vinyl, with a vinyl pathway running the length of the unit. High furniture placed along each edge of the vinyl pathway defines the workshop areas, stable style. As the space had previously been two separate classrooms there were two cloakrooms, two sink areas and two doors leading onto the school corridor, one at each end of the unit.

After

The team began the development process in the second half of the summer term by observing how children used the environment, analysing the data, prioritising learning areas and meeting frequently to plan the next course of action. We all agreed that we needed to start from the beginning of the process and should use the five weeks prior to the summer holidays for team dialogue, creating a floor plan, selecting and ordering furniture and auditing resources.

As Physical Development, Personal, Social and Emotional Development and Language and Communication were our priorities, we felt that each workshop area should be a large space, enabling children to move around freely, working on a large and small scale with their peers. This, together with the location of the sinks, windows, vinyl flooring and sockets informed the siting of each workshop area and as we discussed and agreed on the location of each workshop we drew our floor plan. For example, we sited the creative workshop near the sinks by the window to give children as much natural light as possible for their creative learning. We placed the 'Snack and chat' area by the sinks, over the bridge, at the other end of the room as we didn't feel natural lighting was essential for learning in this area.

As the creative workshop was a popular workshop we sited the block and construction workshop, another popular workshop, on opposite sides of the bridge. From our observations we knew that our children frequently transported additional small world resources into the block area and so we sited these two workshop areas beside each other.

The ICT workshop, with its interactive white board, was on the same side of the bridge as the water, sand, malleable area because of the location of our few sockets. We separated these by placing the maths and role-play areas in between and next to the ICT area. We trained children to ensure they had dry hands before starting any activities in the ICT area.

Another priority was to eliminate the 'stable' effect by opening up the environment and removing 'the runway'. We removed the high furniture and placed two drawer units back to back with a table at each end, in the middle of the runway on one side of the bridge, and mirrored this with a circular table on the other side. This immediately eradicated 'the runway' and gave children easy access to their drawers. It provided a space for a central interactive display with tables at different heights for children to use in their learning. Once we had completed our initial floor plan, we identified the pieces of furniture that were fit for purpose and that we wanted to keep. We then selected and ordered the lower level shelving units we would need to store resources, provide space dividers and define the workshops. To save on space and make the workshop areas as large as possible we used double-sided shelving units wherever possible.

After

The furniture that was not appropriate for the indoor space was used effectively either in the outdoor store or offered to other classes in the school. One of our many challenges was to identify four appropriate key group gathering spaces. The book, ICT and small world areas were obvious spaces. The fourth gathering space we decided to site in what was the recessed entrance to the unit and we now use an 'alternative' entrance to the unit. As the recessed space has an internal door it provides a quiet space ideal for any quieter teaching and learning times such as phonics.

We identified which workshop areas required tables and what height they needed to be. We had the legs of a number of tables shortened using an angle grinder and fitted rubber walking stick stoppers to them to meet safety requirements. From our observations of children we also identified what form of seating, if any was required. We have been flexible with the seating in the creative workshop and children can choose to sit on a chair or not.

During the summer holidays the early years unit was completely emptied and cleaned intensively. The opening shelving units and furniture i.e. painting island, spring-loaded drying rack, water and sand trays, tables, chairs and building blocks were positioned according to our floor plan. Having the luxury of time to implement the floor plan and to stand back and reflect meant we could tweak as we were going along. Once the children returned in September there was very little we needed to change.

We selected the continuous provision for each workshop area with a clear purpose in mind and had in depth discussions about the learning we wanted to take place for our Nursery and Reception aged children e.g. in the water area we had five graded transparent cylinders. We planned for a cross-curricular, multi-sensory and multicultural range of resources in each workshop e.g. number candles, recipes, play dough made with herbs, Chinese bowls and chopsticks, microwave and modelling tools in the malleable workshop.

As we have a mixed age group and children with English as an additional language, we used a range of silhouettes, photographs and text to support independent learning. Once the workshops were complete, we took a photo of each one and placed it in the area as a reference tool for children to use when it was time to put things back.

We were really excited to see how our children would respond to the new layout and resources as being part of a unit our Reception children had experienced a year using the previous environment. Their response was exactly what we had hoped for. Their independence, their investigation and creativity, their social skills and their speaking and listening skills immediately rose to another level. They engaged for longer periods of time in workshop areas instead of flitting from one to another. They became much calmer children and gained confidence. It was such a marked improvement that parents, members of staff, HMI and visitors to school commented on the change. It became evident very quickly, through our tracking systems, that children's progress had rapidly accelerated and our end of year data was noticeably higher.

We continue to observe how our children use the workshop areas in order to meet their learning styles and needs, and enhance the areas accordingly. We know we still have further improvements to make as after a recent Ofsted inspection we were graded 'good' across the board, and so now are working towards an 'outstanding' level for our children.

We also observed that fewer children planned to learn outdoors and so that has become our next challenge – to develop our outdoor learning area to the same level.

Case study 2
. . . .

Improving outcomes by engaging with boys in a nursery/children's centre

Martenscroft EEC, Manchester

Over the last few years, ways of engaging boys in writing has been a major source of discussion. A great deal of research has shown that boys can be reluctant writers; many people arguing that they would prefer to opt out of mark-making altogether and instead opt in to more physical activities, particularly those offered outdoors. EYFS Profile results across the country tend to reflect this, with boys on the whole scoring lower than girls within the writing scales.

However, 'reluctance' may not be the most appropriate word to use. It is not necessarily an objection to the writing process itself that boys display. Instead, it is more often the case that what is offered as early mark-making and writing activities within early years settings does not always link into boy's preferred learning styles and interests. Therefore, there is no real impetus for them to begin to write.

The background

As a whole team, commitment had already been made through professional development opportunities and everyday working practices, to invest time and effort in observing and assessing children's interests and the way in which they individually choose to play and learn. Active discussion in team meetings then led to these observations feeding into the planning and resourcing of activities, with practitioners ensuring that the shaping of activities, and the decisions about enhancing resources within the learning environment, took account of the needs of all the children and any particular interests at the time.

A great deal of work had also gone into incorporating as many creative approaches to learning into everyday practice as possible, in order to actively engage all children.

It was, therefore, a natural step to engage the same processes into an exploration of how to engage boys in mark making and early writing development. It rested on the precept that although girls and boys should have equal learning opportunities, if we are truly following their interests and providing for their learning styles, then this does not necessarily mean offering them the same activities. Girls and boys have unique needs and we need to address these within the learning environment that we provide.

As in all good early years settings, role play opportunities were always on offer to the children. In line with their age and stage of development, there was always a 'home area' within the learning environment. Such young children need to be able to play out their own life experiences and feel the security of a known environment.

However, the home area was not always of as much interest to boys, as it was to girls. The decision was therefore taken to experiment with offering alternative role play environments with different themes, those that would perhaps link more to boy's interests.

Suggested themes included a 'Building site' (ideally tied in with the construction area) and a 'Toy shop' (ideally tied in with the maths area or indeed the investigation or exploration area). Children were very much included in the planning and preparation of these areas, which of course involved writing plans, lists, signs etc. They therefore participated in writing at this stage themselves and also saw it being modelled by adults.

When setting up the area, careful thought was put into what resources/scenarios could be set up in order to encourage children to write as part of their play e.g. for the building site:

- **warning signs**

- **rule boards for the building site**

- **orders to building suppliers**

- **lists of jobs**

- **estimates**

Children came up with ideas of their own. How many adults would have suggested a risk assessment? One boy did – and then engaged others in his industrious play! It was amazing what a supply of clipboards sparked off! Dressing-up clothes on offer also add to 'thinking like the real character'.

The Toy shop took on a life of its own too. Yes, there were signs, there were customer orders and receipts, but there were also plans for an intruder alarm – most important for protecting your precious stock!

There are no limits to the role play opportunities that could be developed. These were very much based on 'real life', but there were space missions and alien play too. How about creating a dinosaur dig or a superhero's hideout?

Picture your mark making and writing provision within your setting. Does it centre round one or two areas of the room? Is the provision mainly small paper, books or table top white boards? Are the writing implements stored in pots on shelves or a table? If so, it is probably highly reflective of many of the traditional mark making environments in settings across the country.

Now think of the attributes of young boys. They like to move freely, often boisterously; they don't often sit still or stay long in one place. Sitting at a table would probably not be their chosen option – they would rather be lying full length on the floor to engage with an activity. This could be seen as stereotypical. Of course, not all boys will be as described as above and some girls will fit the descriptions just as well. However, it is generally accepted that boys don't easily fit the expectations of the traditional educational system and therefore to raise achievement, we must change the way we shape the learning environment and the activities on offer to fit their needs.

And this is what happened in the nursery/children's centre. Practitioners took care to ensure that mark making opportunities were provided on a large scale in different areas of the room. For example, large white boards on the floor allowed for children to lay full stretch together and create marks. Perhaps the lack of permanency added to the attraction. Huge rolls of paper taped to the floor attracted collaborative work. Keying into the areas of interest, such as the small world area and providing clipboards (again!) led to building maps.

Boys could also be seen roaming around the environment with writing backpacks on. No longer did they have to remain at a base in order to create their marks – they simply took their writing implements to the place they wanted to be, the place where there was, in their eyes, a reason and impetus to write.

None of these changes or additions to the learning environment were monumental, but they had positive results: boys became much more involved and interested in mark making and writing. Talk around writing became much more apparent. In terms of offering and encouraging writing on a big scale the impact was great, with noticeable changes in engagement and concentration.

Editor's notes

'Personalised learning' is a key phrase of the moment – changing your environment in ways similar to the above is fulfilling the need to ensure you alter your planning and resourcing to fit each child. There is not a 'one size fits all' approach and by observing boys carefully, listening to their talk and feeding off their ideas, we can improve their outcomes significantly and above all inspire them to want to continue to engage and learn in the future.

Case study 3 Developing a pre-school room environment in a day nursery

Kids Unlimited, Timperley, Cheshire

This case study was undertaken in a private nursery setting of a large national nursery group and is presented as an additional aid to those reflecting on how to set up and organise the environment in their pre-school room. The room was part of a new build and the setting's manager was already presented with a range of resources and equipment standard to new nurseries within the group which had loosely been set up in the room.

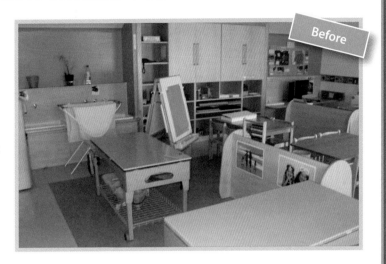

If this book had been written, we could have read it before we started but as it wasn't (you will have the chance to refer to it though!), we relied on what we already knew and felt we needed to achieve for the benefit of the children including:

- **a rich and exciting learning environment for children with a 'wow' factor**

- **an environment that didn't feel dominated by tables and chairs**

- **an inclusive environment that among other things could cater for a child in a wheelchair**

- **an environment that was easily accessible for the children and easily manageable for the adults**

When we had completed our re-organisation we were pleased as we had achieved all our aims and a few more too! We were very much reassured that what had been ordered was in the main fit for purpose and of the right quality and style. We identified what else we needed and arranged to purchase this or put in a request for this to headquarters. But we also come up with some ideas which we felt would further support the setting up of future new nurseries in the group. These ideas included:

- **amending the size of some of the fixed shelving in the large open storage unit so as to more easily accommodate A4 size children's 'Learning Journeys'**

- **ordering some/all the tables with adjustable legs**

- **ordering some different sized tables that could make up a larger table but also be used as a smaller table and at a lower height in some instances (hence the adjustable legs)**

- **ordering some more low level square tables for a variety of uses**

- **creating storage/divider unit ideas mainly for the water/sand areas**

After

We also recognised that it would be necessary to develop child height displays (where possible) and large signage in each area including A4 laminated images with descriptions/comments with existing continuous planning included too. The walls were already painted in neutral colours and floor covering and mats were already what was required.

We started off by identifying which areas we already had represented and those areas we wanted to keep or add. Having done this, we set about deciding where each would be situated. In many cases this meant keeping some in the same place but just re-adjusting the set up (e.g. the book area, ICT area, sand and water, small world and construction areas etc). Once we had decided the size and position, we used masking tape on the floor to delineate these areas and then drew up a large outline sketch.

Our biggest change was to move the role-play area into the centre and a provide a small, child sized gazebo to give this structure a 'wow' factor. Tables were moved into different spaces/areas and at the end we wondered where they all were, such was the new definition we had created.

Editor's notes

The images presented in this case study (before and after) speak for themselves and help to underline the fact that sometimes the most effective changes don't have to cost lots of money just a little time and a little understanding of how children learn best!

After

Chapter 8

Audits for practitioners to reflect on provision and outcomes

These audits are not intended for individual practitioners/leaders and managers to use other than to reflect on practice and provision in general ways. Their main purpose is so that groups of practitioners in settings can come together and use them to focus on self-evaluation of their provision. Although some settings may prefer to fill them in, it is our experience that, unless there is a specific reason for filling them in fully/comprehensively, they are best used as verbal audit tools to support moving practice and provision forward.

They enable whole teams or room teams to engage in sustained shared thinking within a self-evaluation model. Practitioners should remember that self-evaluation starts with celebration (Gould T. 2008) and that we need to identify what we are already doing well and celebrate this and then identify how we can do it even better! This is about ensuring we develop a team vision of what is required to be outstanding and work towards this. The revised EYFS guidance framework (DfE 2012) has a strong focus on the self-reflecting practitioner and these audits will go some way to helping we ensure that this requirement can be effectively met in the areas they cover. It is hoped that settings will use these audits to (among other things):

- **Celebrate existing good practice and ensure this is maintained**

- **Identify growth areas for improving practice**

- **Identify staff training needs and then arrange to meet these**

- **Support effective and strong leadership and management**

- **Ensure that outcomes for all children are consistently good or better**

The audits which follow are:

- **An Emotional Well-being Audit**

- **A Space Audit**

- **A Materials Audit**

- **A Time Audit**

Bibliography & Further Reading

Roberts A. & Featherstone S. (2008) *The Little Book of Treasure Baskets* Featherstone Books

Clarke J. (2007) *Sustained Shared Thinking* Featherstone Books

Cartwright P. Et Al. (2000) *A Place to Learn* Lewisham Early Years

Gould T. (Ed) (2011) *The Fabulous Early Years Foundation Stage* AC Black

Gould T. & Mort L. (2012) *The Little Book of Woodwork* Featherstone Books

Gould T (2012) *Transition In the Early Years* AC Black

Gould T (2012) *Is your EYFS On Track-Self Evaluation Starts With Celebration* AC Black

Osborne A & Melbank J (1987) *The Effects Of Early Education* Clarendon Press

An Emotional Well-being Audit

Aspect	Reflective questions	Description of present position	Further development
Parents/ carers	Is there an effective Key Person system in place?		
	Does your environment reflect the range of languages and cultures reflected in your community?		
	Are there effective transition systems that reflect the needs of your children and parents?		
	Do parents know about these?		
	Are there various ways of communicating with all parents and involving them in their child's education and care?		
	Are parents encouraged to contribute to their child's 'Learning Journey'?		
Peers	Are there a variety of mirrors in the environment to promote a positive self image?		
	Do your children express their feelings?		
	Are children praised, do they know why they are being praised?		
	Do they praise each other?		
	Are your children confident and independent?		

An Emotional Well-being Audit (contd.)

Aspect	Reflective questions	Description of present position	Further development
Peers (contd.)	Do they make choices?		
	Do your children help and comfort each other?		
	Do they play collaboratively, listening to each other's ideas, comments, sharing?		
	Do your children know and talk positively about their culture and beliefs and those of others?		
Practitioners	Do you listen to children, giving them eye contact and time to respond?		
	Do you communicate with each other every day? Are you consistent with your children?		
	Do children share their feelings with you?		
	Do you know each child's learning style, interests, needs, strengths? Do you value each child's efforts?		
	How do you show this?		
	Are you a good role model for your children?		
	Do you have times throughout the day to meet with your key children?		

A Space Audit

Aspect	Reflective questions	Description of present position	Further development
Sufficient	Do you feel a sense of space? Is there optimum space for all children to move around freely? Is there adequate space for children to use the resources creatively on a small and large scale?		
Inviting	Is the furniture fit for purpose and an appropriate height? Is there a range of comfortable seating? Are the resources visible, accessible, multi sensory and open ended? Is there appropriate lighting for the workshop space?		
Caring	Do you know each child's learning style and interest? Does the workshop area meet the needs of all your children? Does the layout, organisation and resourcing of each workshop space reflect your team's thoughts, time, values and vision? Are there plants, drapes, mirrors and lights in your environment?		
Stimulating/ challenging	Are your children involved in sustained shared thinking? Do you become involved in the thinking process with your children? Do children investigate, explore, problem solve, make connections, speculate, predict and ask questions?		

A Space Audit (contd.)

Aspect	Reflective questions	Description of present position	Further development
Flexible	Is there opportunity to rearrange the layout of the furniture, to extend the learning workshop space or add resources in response to children's interests, learning styles and needs?		
Literate	Does each learning workshop space have interactive photographs, signs and labels that encourage a response from children? Are they at the appropriate height for your children? Does the size of the text meet their stages of development? Do your children know what the signs say? Have they been involved in creating some of them? Is there an appropriate amount of text for your children's stages of development?		
Documentation	Is there space at child height to display their learning? Do children have materials to display their learning e.g. magnets, pegs, sticky tack? Are there interactive displays? Have these been modelled/shared? Do some spaces document the learning process? Are informative displays at child height?		

A Materials Audit

Aspect	Reflective questions	Description of present position	Further development
Visible, accessible and clearly labelled	Can your children see each resource on offer? Are they at eye level and within reach? Are the resources displayed in baskets or on open shelving? Are there silhouettes, pictorial and/or text labels to support children's independence? Is there clarity within the workshop?		
Stimulating, challenging and open ended	Can each resource be used in may different ways, stimulating the varying thoughts and ideas children have? Do the resources offer children the opportunity to be creative; to explore, to investigate, to experiment, to problem solve, to be imaginative, to communicate and share their thinking?		
Real objects and tools	Are there real objects in all your workshop areas? Examine each one in turn, reflecting, could some of these resources be replaced by real objects? Do children have access to tools to support their skill development? Have these skills been modelled? Do children have the opportunity to practise and consolidate these skills independently and with practitioners?		
Natural and multi-sensory	Do you have some resources in each workshop for children to look at, to feel, to smell, to stimulate all their senses and draw them into exploration, creativity, investigation and imaginary play?		

A Materials Audit (contd.)

Aspect	Reflective questions	Description of present position	Further development
Recyclable materials	Is there a range of recyclable materials in all workshops?		
	Are they visible and accessible?		
	Are there large and small recyclable materials to construct with?		
	Do you have recyclable materials for pattern making?		
	Do children have access to a basket of recyclable materials to use in their imaginative play?		
Safe, sufficient, clean and in good condition	How often are all the resources audited for safety and quality?		
	Who does the audit?		
	Is it recorded?		
	How often are the resources cleaned?		
	Who cleans them?		
	Are children involved in maintaining resources?		
	Are there systems for ensuring consumables are replenished at the end of each day?		
	Who monitors this to ensure sustainability?		
Multicultural	Are there a range of multicultural resources in each workshop area?		
	Are there multicultural books and images displayed?		

A Time Audit

Aspect	Reflective questions	Description of present position	Further development
Organisation	Has your routine an appropriate balance of time for adult led and child led learning? Is there time for adults to observe children's learning?		
Sufficient	Does your routine of the day allow children longer periods of time in free flow activities for sustained learning, to pursue an idea or interest, to explore, to watch other children, to think or be reflective?		
Flexible	When you observe your children involved in some exciting or sustained deep level learning do you adapt your routine to facilitate this?